This book was published on the occasion of the exhibition
"The Road to Rome" at the Pope John Paul II Cultural Center, Washington, D.C.,
October 2002–May 2003. Curated by Mark Krisco.

POPE JOHN PAUL II
▪ CULTURAL CENTER ▪

The exhibition was sponsored by Marshall Field's and the Target Foundation.

THE ROAD TO
ROME
A MODERN PILGRIMAGE

PAINTINGS AND TEXT BY
FATHER JEROME TUPA

INTRODUCTION BY MARK KRISCO
PHOTOGRAPHS BY BART BARTHOLOMEW

WELCOME BOOKS

NEW YORK & SAN FRANCISCO

[ABOVE] *Rome: Teatro di Marcello*, oil on canvas, 59 x 48 inches.

[PAGE 1] *Rome: Trajan's Column*, pen and ink.

[PAGES 2–3] *Rome: Composite*, oil on canvas, 140 x 73 inches.

[PAGES 4–5] *Rome: Santa Cecilia*, oil on canvas, 60 x 42 inches.

Contents

Published in 2002 by Welcome Books,
An imprint of Welcome Enterprises, Inc.
6 West 18th Street, New York, NY, 10011
(212) 989-3200; Fax (212) 989-3205
email: info@welcomebooks.biz
www.welcomebooks.biz

Publisher: Lena Tabori
Project Director: Katrina Fried
Designer: Gregory Wakabayashi
Design Assistant: Stacey Park

Distributed to the trade in the U.S. and Canada by
Andrews McMeel Distribution Services
Order Department and Customer Service: (800) 223-2336
Orders Only Fax: (800) 943-9831

Library of Congress Control Number:
2002069998

Printed in Italy by Arti Grafiche Amilcare Pizzi, Milan

First Edition
1 3 5 7 9 10 8 6 4 2

For my mother in her 100th year,
for my community of St. John's Abbey,
and for my many companions who have helped me on this great journey.

Blessings and peace to you all!

PREPARATION

Like a deer that yearns for running streams, so my soul longs for you my God! I want my spirit to be carried by a current which is outside of myself. That movement should take me beyond my walls to encounter the Other. So I step out in a search on a road to the heart of belief: the road to Rome.

—FROM THE JOURNAL OF FATHER JEROME TUPA

LIVING IN THE AMERICAN MIDWEST, and being a priest-monk of the Order of Saint Benedict, means that life is rather monochromatic and predictable. The colors of my surroundings are green and blue in the summer; white and shades of gray in the winter. Of course the vestments change a bit with the seasons—from black monks' habits to gray down coats. But planning a pilgrimage to Italy offers a rainbow of possibilities.

This trip is to be a spiritual journey, as seen in the paintings, drawings and reflections of an Italy imbued with da Vinci panoramas and houses colored as if by a Del Sarto. It is meant to be an adventure into the heart of culture and religion, through pictures and prayers. It's meant to open your eyes and heart to some of the new sights and ideas that saints Benedict, Francis, Clare and Catherine knew and loved as part of God's great gifts. Yes, they also saw art, and lots of it.

Preparation begins by considering the obvious form of transport at the end of the millennium: the jet plane. (You maybe expected mules?) Now I know that many people are used to airline travel, but I'm not. For one thing, I am not small. So riding in one of those beasts is a test of patience and serenity. I think that any pilgrimage that begins with a plane ride needs a very strong prayer that somehow God will send the angels to accompany us and hold us up or, once inside the cabin, hold us down. I found out long ago that alcohol does nothing to relieve the pain—in fact, it creates other problems. Prayer is of course the best solution. I don't really trust airplanes, as they are counter-nature. I don't believe in physics. Airplanes can only fly with the help of angels and everyone knows that. Pilots only steer. I recall some of those painful moments on a transatlantic flight when the whole plane would shake and I knew that someone had let down the team and stopped thanking the angels for their fine work.

So as I begin this trip I plan on preparing with prayer. I think a novena to several saints of impossible causes might be invoked. But then again, all of the saints and their enshrined bones that we will visit on this journey might suffice: saints Benedict, Scholastica, Nicholas, Francis, Clare, Anthony and Catherine. They will see us through thick and thin, even Italy in the high summer season, rife and bustling as it is with tourists and vacationers.

I am looking forward to experiencing what pilgrims have experienced for two thousand years. I am going to pray at the great shrines of Christendom. Along the way, I'll do plenty of sitting in piazzas and fields, drawing or painting so you, dear reader, can see where I'm traveling. And hopefully, I will experience a deepening of the Spirit that lives in us all. Maybe you will too.

FATHER JEROME TUPA

THE PILGRIMAGE OF A MONK
THE JOURNEY OF A PAINTER

Painting, like spirituality, is liberating. Both are expressions of one's distinct and deeper relationships with the world—and with God.

—FATHER JEROME TUPA

FATHER JEROME TUPA IS A BENEDICTINE MONK, priest and professor of French at St. John's Abbey/University in Collegeville, Minnesota. He is also an artist, or more specifically, a painter. His artistic path officially began in the early 1970s. For him art was "part of the way of finding balance between the ordered, sane, doctrinaire life of the monastery—where the underpinnings are actually liberating—and the need to express myself."

In the summer of 1999, Father Tupa was inspired to embark on a pilgrimage which began in Milan and ended in Rome. He followed the pilgrim's traditional path through Italy, stopping at many of the ancient, sacred sites and shrines along the way to pay tribute to Christian martyrs and saints. Fortunately for us, he also decided to document his experiences of the Italian countryside and its architecture. The result— a series of three hundred works in oil, watercolor, pen, ink and pencil— shows his clear gift for artistic expression.

Although this pilgrimage dates back to the fourth century, Father Tupa's works are distinctly modern. His creation process bridges history, beginning with the departure from, and ending with the return to, Collegeville, Minnesota. Yet his arrival home marked only the beginning of his artistic journey: the watercolors and drawings created during the pilgrimage were simply the starting points for the expansive works in oil that he had yet to paint. Facing the vast and intimidating white wilderness of a newly primed canvas, Father Tupa began a journey of interpretation, as he sought to translate his remembered experiences into colors, shapes, forms and textures.

In the ancient Italian landscapes, paths and buildings encountered on his pilgrimage, Father Tupa immediately felt the presence of an intense energy and spirit. These sites were linked to an ineffable sense of time, telling stories as old as history. Yet Father Tupa is not the kind of painter who attempts to express such stories by mimicking ancient surfaces in the highly descriptive style so typical of super-realism. Instead, he conveys both the boastfully proud presence of an Italian edifice, and its ungraspable though palpable spiritual presence by keeping his paintings in flux. Fluid, moving patterns of color, form, shape and texture are ultimately and precisely defined by his energized brushstrokes. The spirit of the architecture

[OPPOSITE] Father Jerome Tupa sits and sketches in the great colonnade that surrounds St. Peter's square.

embedded in his memory and noted in his watercolors and drawings fuses with the artist-monk's own spiritual energy and painterly mind. As Father Tupa himself notes, the results are indeed "liberating!"

I.
A RETURN TO THE WELL:
THE MEANING OF PILGRIMAGE

If you came this way, taking any route, starting from anywhere, at any time or at any season, it would always be the same; you would have to put off sense and notion. You are not here to verify, instruct yourself, or inform curiosity or carry report. You are here to kneel where prayer has been valid. And prayer is more than an order of words, the conscious occupation of the praying mind, or the sound of the voice praying. And what the dead have no speech for, when living, they can tell you, being dead: the communication of the dead is tongued with fire beyond the language of the living.

—T. S. ELIOT, *FOUR QUARTETS: LITTLE GIDDING*

IN *IMAGE AND PILGRIMAGE IN CHRISTIAN CULTURE*, one of a series of lectures on the history of religions, sponsored and published by the American Council of Learned Societies, Victor and Edith Turner identified four primary types of pilgrimage: prototypical, archaic, medieval and modern (or rather post-medieval). Prototypical pilgrimages, which continue to be popular, are connected to organized religions: Christians make the pilgrimage to Rome and Jerusalem; Muslims, to Mecca; Sikhs, to Ammritsar; Hindu, to Kumba Meta and Mount Kailas; Mormons, to Salt Lake City; and Buddhists, to Kandy and Kyoto. The archaic pilgrimage includes, for example, the Celtic pilgrimages to Glastonbury or Pennant Melangell

near Llangynog in mid-Wales. The medieval pilgrimages are those which took place between 500–1400.

While people continue to pilgrimage for religious reasons, "praying with their legs" as the expression goes, other contemporary pilgrimages are made for non-religious purposes. One embarks on this kind of a journey as an act of thanksgiving, penance, healing—for oneself, a family member, or a friend. One can also undertake an artistic pilgrimage, stopping at well-known museums where art and artifacts are revered as if they were religious relics. Then too, there are historic pilgrimages, during which one might tour major military battlefields and cemeteries. Finally, there are those who take pilgrimages that have "religious" connotations for non-religious reasons. The actress Shirley MacLaine made such a journey to Santiago de Compostela, in search of the spirit and energy—specifically the ley lines—of the earth, which are said to induce "clarity of thought, experience, memory and revelation."

Regardless of categories and regardless of reasons, one fact remains constant. A pilgrimage is a physical journey that is taken for metaphysical reasons. It is a return to the well, as it were, that quenches the spirit and refreshes the soul. When a pilgrim steps out, he leaves behind the familiar in search of something that has somehow been mislaid or lost. Frequently, this is an individual's sense of belonging, which is why pilgrimages, by their very nature, put the pilgrim in the company of other like-minded travelers. Although they may be strangers from different parts of the world, they share a common purpose. Likewise, they may follow different religions, but remain united in a journey that requires the same leap of faith in all of them. And truthfully, no map, no list of sites, no guide to shrines or cities can trace their true journey or destination. Despite the original goals and the various difficulties encountered along the way, the pilgrim is always rewarded with the knowledge that his quest is inherently good. As Catherine of Siena said, "All the way to Heaven is heaven." Ultimately, only this approach can free the pilgrim's spirit.

Although there is mention of pilgrimages throughout the Old Testament, the true era of Christian pilgrimage began after the death of Jesus Christ, when many of his followers began to secretly meet at the tombs of the early martyrs and saints in Rome. In A.D. 313, Emperor Constantine established Christianity as the Imperial religion and in 325, his mother Helena set out for Jerusalem on a pilgrimage to visit the ancient sites. Upon her return, Emperor Constantine began erecting churches and basilicas throughout Christendom.

Pilgrims in the west continued to travel to Rome primarily to visit the tombs of Peter and Paul. During the predominantly Christian Middle Ages, pilgrimages, especially those to Marian shrines (to pay tribute to the Madonna) thrived. In these years, roughly between A.D. 500 and 1500 the so-called "pilgrim highways" began to develop, replete with hospices and accommodations. Of the more famous are Santiago de Compostela, Rome, Walsingham, Zaragoza, Loug Derg and Loreto. Christian pilgrimage remained popular until the sixteenth century when Protestant reformers, believing that pilgrimage violated their concept "of faith alone," discouraged pilgrimages and called them "useless journeys."

Interior of St. Peter's Basilica.

Though the spiritual value of pilgrimage was reaffirmed by Pope Paul III during the counter Reformation of the mid-sixteenth century, the number of pilgrimages was still below that of the Middle Ages. Then, with multiple appearances of the Blessed Virgin Mary, all that changed. Marian shrines were quickly erected at the sighting locales and became the destinations of many new pilgrimages. Chief among these sites were: Rue de Bac (1830)—which involved Saint Catherine Labouré; La Salette (September 19, 1846)—involving two children; Lourdes—where there were eighteen apparitions reported between February 11 and July 16, 1858 involving Bernandette Soubirous; Pontmain (January 17, 1871)—which involved four children; and finally, Pellevision—where there were fifteen apparitions between February 14 and December 8, 1876. Two twentieth-century apparitions again produced a dramatic increase in pilgrimages, when, in Banneaux, nine apparitions were reported between January 1933 and February 1, 1934, and in Beauraing, another nine apparitions were reported between November 29, 1932 and January 3, 1933. During the years immediately following both series of sitings, nearly seven thousand pilgrims traveled to these two locales alone.

In the mid 1960s, the Second Vatican Council issued its "Call to Holiness," inspiring millions to embark on pilgrimages. For example, the number of pilgrimages made to Lourdes alone tripled during this period. Today, besides the earlier mentioned Marian shrines, there are seven other pilgrimage sites popular among Christians: Czestochowa in Poland; El Rocio and Santiago de Compostela in Spain (Andalucia); Our Lady of Fatima in Portugal; Jerusalem; Rome; and Saint Anne de Beaupre in Canada (Quebec). Given the ease and relatively low cost of modern transportation, pilgrimages will no doubt continue to grow steadily. In Europe, for instance, the number of pilgrimages has risen to an impressive twenty million.

II.
THE PILGRIMAGE PAINTINGS: ON THE ROAD AND AT HOME

FATHER JEROME TUPA'S *ROAD TO ROME* ARTWORK unfolded in a two-part experience that owes itself to reasons of practicality. Initially, it emerged in the form of the drawings and watercolors created during the pilgrimage itself—completed on location in lightweight portable sketchbooks and on conventionally-sized watercolor paper. Then, upon his return home, Father Tupa began the mural-sized oil paintings, which are not only massive, but required extended periods of time to execute, impossible on a pilgrimage where daily travel is a necessity.

All of these pieces (drawings, watercolors and oils) are self-sufficient works of art in and of themselves. Of the drawings, a great many are as sensitively composed and aesthetically satisfying as the watercolors, which are themselves exquisite. On occasion a watercolor is used to create an oil painting, though the drawings tend to con-

Rome: The Piazza della Rotonda, watercolor, 38 x 28 inches.

Rome: The Piazza della Rotonda, oil on canvas, 59 x 48 inches.

tain more of the seeds of that process, and an oil painting may be based on more than one.

So, while our personal aesthetic might lead us to prefer either the watercolors and drawings or the oils, to exclude one for the other would be to miss the totality of the pilgrimage experience and creative process. Listening to the melody of an opera without its accompanying words can be enjoyable, but only by listening to the whole score—music and libretto alike—do we hear the entire sound as the composer intended. The complete resonance comes from the artistic process of exploiting the inherent and contrasting natures of these complementary media.

Once back in the studio, Father Tupa has the advantage of being stationary and private once again, conditions which allow him to greatly increase the size of his pieces. And in turn, working on a mural scale enables him to match the ambition and energy of the great frescos and mosaics he surely studied on his Italian pilgrimage. Ultimately, the dueling media of Father Tupa's artistic journey is a coin toss: the "heads" of his watercolors and drawings are necessary as much as the "tails" of his oil paintings.

The qualities of Father Tupa's dueling media, and the conditions under which they were conceived, also contribute to our enjoyment of these works. In the watercolors, Father Tupa uses the transparent nature of the medium to create delicately airy paintings; this transparency belies the fact that the artist's chief pursuit when working in watercolor is sunlight—which is, essentially, ephemeral. Having been completed "en plein air," the watercolors are more naturalistic and generally less abstract than the oils. Also, the watercolors primarily deal with landscapes, even when not pure landscapes—i.e. those in which buildings are inserted into a landscape scene.

In contrast, the oils are dynamically abstract, opaque and exceedingly more inventive. In part, these qualities emerge from the freedom Father Tupa feels in the privacy of his studio. Not being in the field—perhaps no longer inhibited by curious passersby—he can paint with more dramatic strokes and colors. This element, along with the luxuries of time and scale, stir within Father Tupa the desire, and the need, to improvise.

While the watercolors pursue transient light and at times pure landscape, the pilgrimage oils primarily explore architecture—structures solidly planted on terra firma—but in an abstracted, compelling way. These paintings often depict buildings that swell and sway—towers and campaniles seem to bend to fit within the frame. This is done by Father Tupa to convey to the viewer a sense of the true height and massive scale of such structures. Father Tupa's leaning church domes and towers have a painterly integrity. The artist is well aware of the presence of photography and the prevalence of postcards, and realizes that his job is not to make a literal record. His job, rather, is to create a living—and therefore literally moving—symbolically emotional entity. To do so, Father Tupa must enter into communion with his materials, and improvise on the canvas—an activity that he doubtlessly understands well, from his experience as a Benedictine monk. And to quote a jazz great, the violinist Stephane Grappelli, "Great improvisers are like priests; they are only thinking of their god." During the process of improvisation, Father Tupa imbues his paintings with the energy and ability to greatly effect how we experience the sacred or secular buildings they depict. But in this painter's hands, all the architecture along the road to Rome becomes sacred in an aesthetic sense. It's a sacredness that emerges out of the intermingling of the painter's focused yet playful state; his chosen strident, vivid palette; the dramatically lit and dynamic forms he has chosen to explore; and the large format and scale of the work.

While not interested in realism, Father Tupa tailors the degree of improvisation to the nature of the building he is portraying. In *Florence: The Duomo*, for instance, the painting conveys the maternal stability of the structure. In this work Father Tupa extends that sense of stability by balancing the predominantly "cool" center of the street and church with a flanking of "hot" buildings on either side. The scale of the duomo then gradually increases, along with the size of the triangular cap-like roofs, which also give the impression of stability. In contrast, the only sense of stability conveyed in *Loreto: the Holy House* is the horizon, located along the upper third of the work. Meanwhile the Holy House itself seems to sway and dance, suggesting not only its miraculous and legendary ability to transport itself, but the possibility that it may actually move itself yet again.

These observations suggest this: each component of Father Tupa's artistic journey contributes a deeper understanding to our appreciation of both his pilgrimage and his creative travels as well. Taken together, his light and airy watercolor landscapes and drawn delineations of architecture, completed in situ, and his visually tactile and rhythmically playful oils, done in the studio, help us to kinesthetically feel the spirit of these ancient and sacred places.

[ABOVE] Drawings 1A, 1B and 1C of San Gimignano.
[BELOW] *San Gimignano: Summer Heat*, oil on canvas, 76 x 64 inches.

III.
FROM DRAWING TO PAINTING: THE ARTIST'S JOURNEY

The *Road to Rome* works are painterly and abstracted improvisations on one or more drawings from two large, leather-bound sketchbooks Father Tupa carried with him on his pilgrimage. A closer examination of this process of translation helps us appreciate the artist's powers of invention, which in turn furthers our understanding of the spirituality Father Tupa felt at these sites.

The oil *San Gimignano: Summer Heat* was painted from four drawings. The first (1A) provides the oil with its massive central foreground pillar. While the pillar in the drawing seems oriented towards the front, the pillar in the painting seems oriented on a slight diagonal. This shift is further enhanced by the diagonal wedge of shadow running across the central foreground. The second drawing (1B) provides us with the literal appearance of the buildings, as seen in the distant center building. Yet, when we compare the multiple towers between drawing and painting, we

find them in the drawing to be stretched out like fingers reaching for the sky. In contrast, the third drawing (1C) depicts the tower seen, in the oil version, on the right. In both versions, the towers appear to bend. However, while the drawing's tower appears to be bent so as to fit the sketchbook page, the bent tower in the oil serves the pur-

Padova: Onion Domes, drawing 2A (left) and oil on canvas, 40 x 46 inches (right).

pose of moving the eye through the much-expanded vista within this larger frame. This particular painting is further enhanced by the addition of the figure with a crutch, adding a precise sense of scale, and suggesting the day's intense heat. Ultimately, this oil and *San Gimignano: The Towers*, done from a single drawing, place the emphasis on the numerous medieval towers for which this commune of Siena is known.

The oil *Padova: Onion Domes* is born of the overlapping information of a drawing (2A) and a watercolor of similar title. As in the San Gimignano works, this drawing presents the building to us frontally. But, as before, the artist immediately shifts this orientation onto the diagonal in the oil. This suggests that, when confronted with a long rectangular canvas, the artist has been compelled to stretch the dimensions of the building as well. And quite

unusually, notice that the artist has taken more abstract liberties with the watercolor version of this work, while the oil version exploits the full girth of the "onion" shaped towers.

The oil *Lucca: The Duomo* illustrates both the characteristics already discussed: the artist shifts the building to a diagonal orientation (3B), and the leaning tower within the work is already bent in the drawn version (3A). But here, the bending tower is switched to the opposite side of the entrance doors. And, having heavily shaded the doorways and tower (3A), Father Tupa obviously understood the importance of the building's three-dimensionality. Again he adds even more space to his oil by introducing a landscape space stretching far back into the distance on both sides of the duomo.

A similar dramatic altering of fact can be seen in

Lucca: The Duomo, drawings 3A and 3B (left and center) and oil on canvas, 93 x 42 inches (right).

Florence: The Duomo, one of the few paintings where the central building, the duomo, has a similar frontal orientation to the drawings (4A and 4B). By maintaining this frontal orientation, Father Tupa conveys the duomo's grand presence and stability. But he has also simplified the facts by omitting the second story of the restaurant on the right side. Here, without the option of adding landscape space on either side, Father Tupa instead inserts a shrine, on the left, and a tower behind it.

The last painting completed in the *Road to Rome* series, *Orvieto*, has one of the most elongated rectangle formats in the entire group. Not surprising then, is the fact that it required the information from five drawings (5A–5E) to create. These drawings range from closely focused facade details (5C and 5D) to drawings that zoom out to include part of the street. In the oil, Father Tupa decided to include the cars and figures evident in the drawings (5A and 5B), knowing that their presence was

Florence: The Duomo, drawings 4A and 4B (left and center) and oil on canvas, 64 x 76 inches (right).

Drawings 5A–5E of Orvieto, which were combined to serve as the basis for the final oil painting.

integral to his description of the building itself. Looking at drawings 5A and 5E, the viewer will also notice that Father Tupa needed to bend the building on the right side. Most importantly, Father Tupa makes his central focus the ornate thirteenth-century facade. In the end, the oil ends up being composed like a sentence, with the central buildings being noun, verb and adjective punctuated with the "commas" of figures and cars, and flanked by buildings on either side that act, in a sense, like parentheses.

As the above comparisons reveal, Father Tupa does indeed take artistic liberties with the architecture depicted in his *Road to Rome* series. These are liberties that any painter might take, if that painter requires the viewer to respect the abstract translation of a three-dimensional world onto the flat surface of the canvas. In his series, Father Tupa accomplishes this task with a refreshing and ever-changing dialogue between what is depicted and how it is depicted. This painterly play instills our interest and delight in the color, forms, textures and light of Italy.

Orvieto, oil on canvas, 93 x 42 inches.

[ABOVE] Father Jerome sketching the Tiber Island in Rome.
[OVERLEAF] *Rome: The Tiber Island*, three panels, oil on canvas, 90 x 36 inches.

IV.
THE ROAD TO ROME:
THE LONG VIEW

We shall not cease from exploration and the end of all our exploring will be to arrive where we started and to know the place for the first time.
— T. S. ELIOT, *FOUR QUARTETS: LITTLE GIDDING*

FATHER TUPA'S OILS, WATERCOLORS AND DRAWINGS in the *Road to Rome* series are composed of individual interpretative compositions of Italian architecture and landscape. Yet they are so geographically and stylistically similar, we could view them as one work. This fact recalls to my mind the words of Stanley I. Grand in the catalog *The Tuscany Landscape of Richard Upton*: "The paintings, linked together like rosary beads, become a mantra for meditation." Father Tupa's style, with its consistent palette, forms and rhythms, presents us with the visual invitation to participate in his journey. If we accept, his journey will compel us to contemplate our own journeys, for, whether we travel around the world or stay closer to home, we are all in some way pilgrims on a pilgrimage.

As pilgrims then, we all progress by learning. Life is nothing so much as a series of lessons which, when learned, act as keys to the doorways of our souls, and our life force. These lessons ultimately teach us to be better people, capable of embracing all of creation. For as the Taoist Lao Tzu said, "The master is available to all people and doesn't reject anyone. He is ready to use all situations and doesn't waste anything. This is called embodying the light."

So let us be thankful for Father Tupa's *Road to Rome* pilgrimage, and the resulting works of art, for they offer us the possibility of just such enlightenment.

MARK KRISCO, *Exhibition curator*

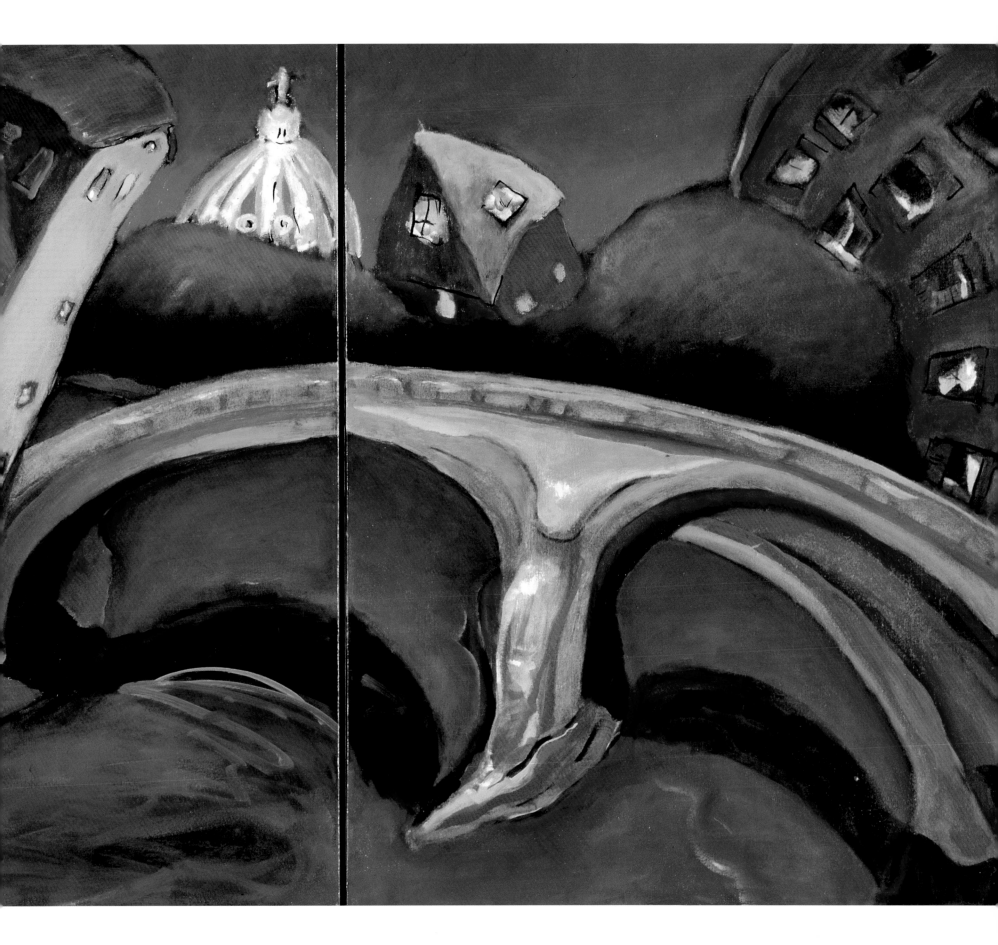

THE JOURNEY BEGINS

MILAN

LOVING GOD OF THE JOURNEY

YOU GIVE US MARKERS ALONG THE WAY

TO GUIDE, TO LEAD, TO COMFORT, TO INSTRUCT

WE BLESS YOU FOR AMBROSE OF MILAN

WHOSE WISDOM AND HOLINESS

LED MANY TO PRAISE AND FOLLOW YOU

GRANT THAT WE MAY GAIN WISDOM AND A CARING HEART

THAT WE MIGHT PRAISE YOU WITH GREAT FERVOR

AMEN

FEW VISITORS TO MILAN ARE AWARE that this cosmopolitan center of high fashion, banking, industry and the arts has such a remarkable history, but this northern Italian city dates back more than two millennia. It was settled in the fourth century B.C. by Gallic Celts, and quickly became known as Mediolanum, referring to the fact that even then the town was "in the middle of things."

Ever expanding its hold on the Italian peninsula, Rome conquered the Celts and annexed Mediolanum in 222 B.C. By 52 B.C. the rustic settlement had developed into a major Roman municipality, and was the staging center for military forays against the barbarian peoples of the north.

In A.D. 286, the seat of the Western Roman Empire was transferred from Rome to Mediolanum; soon it was second only to Rome in both size and importance. It functioned as the capital until A.D. 402, when Emperor Honorius established Ravenna on the Adriatic Sea as the capital of the Empire of the West.

For the Christian visitor or pilgrim, Milan has major significance, or ought to. Already an important Christian center in the early fourth century, it was from this city that the Emperor Constantine, fresh from his decisive victory over his political rival Maximian at Rome's Milvian Bridge, issued the pivotal Edict of Milan in A.D. 313. The edict granted Christianity the status of "tolerated

[OPPOSITE] *Milan: San Ambrosia*, oil on canvas, 42 x 60 inches.

religion" within the Roman Empire and was indisputably one of Christianity's defining moments, for better or for worse. It enabled Christians to legally assemble, organize a hierarchical structure of church governance, and erect buildings for worship and gatherings. But the imperial patronage also meant that many people now sought to be baptized as Christians not out of religious conviction, but because it was the politically appropriate thing to do. Convenience replaced conviction in many cases, much to the detriment of the Church.

If Constantine was primarily responsible for Christianity's new legal status, the fourth-century bishop of Milan, Ambrose, was primarily responsible for the faith's prodigious flowering and maturation. An imperial functionary designated as bishop by Milan's faithful, Ambrose quickly gained the respect and reverence of the Roman world. He attracted people from every corner of the empire to his diocese, be they pagans or Christian believers.

Perhaps none among Ambrose's disciples is better known than Augustine of Hippo in Roman North Africa. Augustine would later be acknowledged as one of the Church's greatest saints, and was a Doctor of the Church much like his mentor. A former practitioner of heretical Arian Christianity, he was converted by Ambrose to the Catholic faith then embraced by most Western Christians, and baptized by Ambrose himself.

Ambrose dedicated himself tirelessly to the establishment and strengthening of the faith in his diocese. He was known as a matchless teacher, eloquent preacher, compassionate pastor, accomplished administrator, liturgist, scholar, and saint. Under his direction the Milanese church took on much of the same structure that defines it to this day, both architecturally and spiritually.

In fact, much of the church architecture familiar to or built by Ambrose still exists in Milan. A fact which may well strike pilgrims as strangely incongruous is that in Milan one finds fourth-century churches alongside twentieth-century corporate headquarters. But while the latter tend to concern themselves with worldly treasures, the churches of Milan house sacred relics as precious as any earthly treasure to Christian pilgrims.

If Saint Ambrose is arguably Milan's greatest Christian figure, then to visit the church housing his relics is surely one of the primary goals for Christian pilgrims in Milan. The great Doctor of the Church is buried in the crypt of the Basilica of Saint Ambrose (which Ambrose himself built), in a glass-sided casket. His bodily remains are still clothed in a bishop's vestments.

Significantly, Saint Ambrose is not buried alone in his own basilica, but humbly shares the church's crypt, and his own casket, with two other famous Milanese saints: Gervase and Protase, reputedly sons of Saints Vilate and Valeria. Gervase and Protase were considered two of the earliest and greatest leaders of the fledgling Christian community at Mediolanum; they died gloriously as martyrs for the Christian faith before it was legally tolerated. During one of his numerous construction projects, Ambrose discovered the martyrs' graves in an early Christian cemetery outside the city walls. He had their relics carried triumphantly to his basilica, where they still rest, one on each side of the sainted bishop.

Milan was blessed with yet another sainted bishop in the sixteenth century, Charles Borromeo, who was born into a noble Italian family related to the famous Medicis, and was the nephew of a pope. Charles entered the service of the Church at the age of twelve, when he received the clerical tonsure. He rose quickly in the ecclesiastical ranks and was soon named a cardinal. He was then appointed to the lofty position of Papal Secretary of State, much to his dismay—for his greatest desire was to live a life dedicated to holiness, totally committed to the love of Christ and the care of Christ's faithful.

Milan: Four Arches, watercolor, 29³/₄ x 22¹/₈ inches.

For years this good man humbly submitted to the commands of the pope and worked wholeheartedly on the many assignments entrusted to his care. The enormous joy that Charles experienced when he was named archbishop of the ancient Church of Milan was one that he obediently set aside for a number of years until he could finally persuade the pope to release him from his duties in Rome. When the absentee Archbishop Charles was at last able to journey to Milan and take possession of his cathedral, he became that city's first resident archbishop in over eighty years. The Milanese faithful received him with delirious acclaim; Charles never disappointed them.

If Martin Luther is, in the popular view, the religious figure most identified with the Catholic Church's reformation from without, Charles Borromeo deserves similar recognition as the religious figure most committed to the Church's reformation from within. He was a tireless, matchless reformer. Commissioned by the pope to reconvene the long-adjourned Council of Trent and the subsequent implementation of its reforming decrees, he traveled long distances throughout Italy and southern Europe in order to oversee the reform of the higher clergy, in particular. He never asked anything of a fellow bishop or priest that he was not willing to do himself.

Despite his exalted rank, he lived in absolute simplic-

Milan: Sant' Ambrogio Bell Tower, watercolor, 29½ x 21¹⁵/₁₆ inches.

Milan: Sant' Andrea, watercolor, 30¼ x 22 inches.

Milan: Duomo, pen and ink.

ity, and his charity and genuine concern for the neediest members of his flock were legendary. When the dreaded plague struck Milan and its surrounding countryside, it was Charles who voluntarily went to the aid of the poorest of the poor, and nursed those most severely afflicted by the deadly disease. His exemplary ministry became the most convincing of arguments for his frightened clergy, who eventually imitated his fearless example and came to the assistance of Milan's sick and dying. Having lived and died as the most beloved of Milan's spiritual fathers since Saint Ambrose himself, he was buried in the city's fourteenth-century Gothic cathedral. There, his tomb is among the most sacred of destinations. The cathedral, or duomo, is a magnificent structure, the largest and most elaborate Gothic building in all of Italy.

It houses other major Christian relics, precious to the faithful, as well—in particular, one of the holy nails used to crucify Christ to his cross on Calvary. The relics were originally found by Emperor Constantine's mother, Saint Helena, in the course of her excavations in Jerusalem as she sought the true cross and other sacred relics related to Christ's birth, life, death and resurrection. Helena purportedly gave the holy nails to her son, and one of those nails was brought from Rome to Milan by Saint Ambrose himself.

Another particularly notable set of celebrated Milanese relics (especially to pilgrims) is the bodily remains of the Magi, the Three Wise Men. These sacred relics are said to have been discovered in the city's primitive Christian cemetery. They were housed in the church of Sant' Eustorgio

5:30 a.m.: I'm off to the duomo to draw. Now here is one big late-medieval church. The carvings are so finely rendered that they have the appearance of lace. There is so much stone carved as something celestial that I find it difficult to see this as a real prayer space. I'm in awe, and that is good. It is an earthly awe that keeps me grounded, and doesn't lead me deeper into prayer or devotion.

The visit to Saint Ambrose's tomb seems to suspend time. Ambrose influenced such people as Saint Augustine, and because of his writings, he is perhaps one of the most important figures in the early Church. As I reflect on Saint Ambrose and his impact on Christianity I look around at the people praying in this church. We have all been touched by our neighbors and family, both living and dead. How often I think of my grandparents and their role in my religious education. In my small church, the patron saint was Bridget, and I never could understand the importance of this person for our parish. Here in Milan, however, I begin thinking of the saint who actually walked these streets and helped form the very foundation of the faith here in northern Italy. This man lived within the walls of a town that knew him as a valued citizen. As the church proclaimed him holy and sanctified, the people who lived here could still remember him as someone who had been a neighbor, yet was now also one of the blessed in heaven. So his bones lying here in this shrine are still those of a neighbor. He is not some distant mythical character.

until A.D. 1164, when they were forcibly removed and transferred to the Cathedral of Cologne, Germany, by the Imperial Chancellor Rinaldo, who was reportedly acting on the explicit orders of Emperor Frederick Barbarossa. But the loss of the Magi's relics was a severe blow to the faithful of Milan, and caused great antipathy toward the northerners who had absconded with them.

It was thus a time for great rejoicing and reconciliation when, in 1904, the cardinal archbishop of Milan, Andrea Ferrari, in a solemn ritual, restored a portion of the relics to Sant' Eustorgio. Appropriately enough, the celebration took place on the Feast of the Epiphany (Three Kings' Day). It was Cologne's Cardinal Archbishop Anton Fischer who personally made the transfer possible. In return, a grateful Cardinal Ferrari presented to him a cope and rosary that had been used by another of Milan's Archbishops, Saint Charles Borromeo.

Bobbio, watercolor, 29 3/4 x 22 3/16 inches.

BOBBIO

HOME OF SAINT COLUMBANUS

JUST AS YOU ACCOMPANIED THE HOLY MONK COLUMBANUS
ON THE SEARCH FROM IRELAND TO ENGLAND,
AND FINALLY TO ITALY,
FOR WORTHY SPIRITS TO CARRY YOUR MESSAGE OF LOVE,
CONTEMPLATION, AND PRAYER FOR ALL CITIZENS OF THE WORLD,
BE WITH US, AND FILL US WITH SPIRIT—
THAT WE MAY SHOW THE INNER LIGHT THAT CAN BRING
JUSTICE AND PEACE TO ALL WE MEET.

FAR FROM THE CONVENTIONAL ROUTE of most casual sight-seers is the strikingly picturesque and revered town of Bobbio. Bobbio has particular meaning for Christian pilgrims, as it shelters the shrine of a saint who could easily lay claim to the title "Father of all Christian pilgrims": Saint Columbanus (c. 525–615).

To follow the trail of this Irish monk, pilgrim, missionary and religious founder to Bobbio is to review, as if in miniature, much of Europe's early Christian history.

Columbanus represents a breed of early western monastics little known or appreciated today. The "father of western monasticism," the influential Italian Benedict of Nursia (c. 480–547), emphasized the importance of "stability of place" for monks living in community, and condemned monks who wandered. But the Irish monks highlighted the religious value of the *peregrinatio pro Domino*, or the "pilgrimage for the sake of the Lord." It was within the penitential framework of early Irish monasticism, characterized by its austere nature, that the custom of *peregrinatio pro Domino* developed. In practice, monastic men and women would commit themselves—often through solemn vows or promises—to leave their beloved native land, and all that was near and dear, forever. They embarked on a self-made exile "for the sake of the Lord." There was a deeply religious value to these actions. Underlying their voluntary renunciations was the desire

to exhort other Christians to recognize that "there is no permanent city for us here; we are looking for the one which is yet to be" (Hebrews 13:14); that "our homeland is in heaven and it is from there that we are expecting a savior, the Lord Jesus Christ" (Philippians 3:20), and that we are called to imitate our Lord Jesus, who had "nowhere to lay his head" (Matthew 8:20).

Beyond its ability to so powerfully convey this spiritual lesson, the *peregrinatio pro Domino* bore more practical fruits. The wandering monastic exiles became de facto missionaries, preaching the Gospel of Christ everywhere they went. Their brief sojourns often resulted in the founding of local churches and monasteries, which in turn became important centers of Christian and monastic life and intellectual development. In this guise, Columbanus left his cherished Ireland in 590 to begin his own travels. He journeyed through what are now parts of France, Switzerland and northern Italy. His final stop was Bobbio.

In 614, Columbanus occupied the ruined chapel of San Pietro in Bobbio and began monastic life, attracting an amazingly large number of disciples in a very short time. By the time he died, on November 23, 615, Bobbio contained a well-established community of monks observing the uncompromisingly severe Rule which their holy father had transmitted to them. Columbanus' abbey flourished, becoming a major monastic center and greatly

BOBBIO: 7/5/99

After our departure from Milan, we made a great discovery—the little town of Bobbio. This village is off the radar for today's traveler, but was just what we were looking for. It was one of the major pilgrimage sites of medieval times because of the great Saint Columbanus. The town is a superbly preserved medieval burg built around the tomb of the Saint.

Columbanus was a true pilgrim, arriving in this mountain valley in the fifth century after travelling from Ireland through Great Britain and France down to Italy. His possessions consisted of a sack of small necessities, such as a knife and perhaps a book. His means of transport was the Spirit. Steeped in prayer, it is reported that at each stop he attracted people, who saw his holiness and God's divine love flowing from him.

Today's Bobbio is a jewel of arcades, towers and cobblestone streets, winding every which way up from the riverbed to the monastery. Suspended over the little river is the most crooked bridge I have ever seen. This is art in stone: I had to spend some time drawing and painting here. But the town boasted another treat, breakfast with a fresh cornetto (warm and crusty) and a great cup of coffee. Sitting in the sunshine I watched the Saturday morning market open, with its rainbow of colored flowers, fruits (apricots that were like honey!), vegetables, the smell of roasting chicken on sale at the meat vendor, and wheels of fresh Parmesan and Pecorino. What an aroma! I wonder whether these people know how much beauty surrounds them. Alas, the time came for us to go. So once again we set off to discover the roads of Italy.

Formerly pilgrims would travel together in order to assure their safety and trade news from other villages or countries. They would walk in groups, and find shelter as one big family for many weeks at a time while praying and exchanging ideas and stories. In contrast, a pilgrimage today demands that we take little roads where there is almost no traffic, and few people. But the Italian countryside continues to charm us—with its golden fields, green pastures and dark green-blue mountains, just as it must have for the pilgrims of long ago.

Bobbio: Main Square, watercolor, 30¹/8 x 22¹/8 inches.

enriching the sacred liturgy, learning and the arts. Its contributions to Christian and monastic culture in Europe established it as the northern counterpart of Saint Benedict's southern abbey of Monte Cassino.

As their predecessors did, today's pilgrims come to revere the relics of Saint Columbanus in the basilica now dedicated to him. It was once the abbey church, built where Columbanus and his early disciples prayed and worked, studied and farmed. Within the church's fifteenth-century incarnation lies the much older, ninth-century crypt with the saint's sarcophagus. And while this apparent disparity may temporarily confuse the visitor, the crypt is evidence of just how ancient this site really is, and just how sacred it has been to Christian pilgrims for well over thirteen hundred years.

In this place
Where pilgrims stop on their journeys
To honor the relics of the passion, death and
resurrection of the Lord Jesus
We see and feel with a deep sadness that violence has
its home in our hearts and in our homes.
Lord heal the wounds of hatred and strife.
Bring peace to our world that is searching for your
face of love and mercy.

There are certain cities throughout the world that owe their very existence and importance to some major religious connection or event. To visit them becomes the sacred goal of streams of devout pilgrims. Such is the little-known city of Mantova, in Italy's north central Lombardy region.

Official records from the court of Emperor Charlemagne describe the momentous discovery that led to Mantova's significance. In the year A.D. 804, the relics of "the Most Precious Blood of Our Lord Jesus Christ," together with the body of Saint Longinus—the Roman centurion who pierced Jesus' side with his lance on the hill of Calvary—were uncovered. They had lain hidden in this spot, in the then-inconsequential village of Mantova, for centuries. Pious tradition would later supply the detail that the discovery resulted from the appearance of the Apostle Saint Andrew to a devout Christian.

Pope Leo III is said to have made the lengthy journey from Rome to Mantova at the personal invitation of Charlemagne in order to authenticate these relics. A minuscule portion of the relic of the Precious Blood was then sent to the emperor in Paris, and reverently housed in the Royal Chapel. And Mantova, as the place that sheltered such exalted relics of Christ's Passion, was quickly elevated to the rank of a city. In recognition of its great dignity, it was given its own bishop.

Just how Mantova came to harbor these relics in the first place is explained by the intimate connection between Saint Longinus, the centurion, and the relic of Christ's Precious Blood. The gospel according to John describes Jesus' side being pierced by a lance by "one of the soldiers" (John 19:34). The gospel accounts of Matthew, Mark and Luke refer to the centurion in charge of the Roman soldiers who were responsible for Jesus' crucifixion. Tradition, or rather a popular reading of all four gospels, seems to have conflated the various narratives into a single account. And in this account, the centurion is

A SACRED DESTINATION
MANTOVA

[OPPOSITE] Mantova's Piazza Centrale.

Mantova: Golden Balcony, watercolor, 30¼ x 22¾ inches.

ultimately understood to be the one who in fact pierced Jesus' side with his lance.

In time, the unnamed centurion of the gospels was said to have been called Longinus. At the moment of Jesus' death, he exclaimed, "In truth this man was Son of God" (Mark 15:39), a remark which has come to be interpreted as an act of belief, denoting his conversion to faith in Jesus Christ. The believing and repentant Longinus is said to have then gathered up the blood-soaked soil at the foot of the Cross, as well as the lance-blade with which he himself had pierced Jesus. He carried them with him, treasuring them throughout the course of his life, until he himself died a martyr's death for his Lord.

Mantovan tradition holds that Longinus' martyrdom took place in their own town, which was at that time a minor outpost on the Roman border. The centurion's body was buried by fellow Christians, in the same place where he had previously hidden the relics of the Precious Blood for safekeeping, in anticipation of his death.

No mention, by the way, is ever made of the sacred lance in any of the Mantovan accounts. This omission actually tends to support the veracity of the story, since the sacred lance was said to be preserved in Saint Peter's Basilica in Rome. The lance came to Saint Peter's after one of the Muslim sultans returned it to the Pope in a gesture of good will. An "extra" sacred lance would have "muddied the waters" of Mantova's claims.

The presence of the sacred relics of Jesus' Precious Blood and the remains of Saint Longinus certainly designated Mantova as a major pilgrimage site. Streams of pilgrims flowed into the town, contributing to the city's ever-increasing importance. Population and commerce flourished, with a nearly constant building of new churches, monasteries and housing for the multitudes of

Mantova, watercolor, 30 x 22¹/₄ inches.

visiting pilgrims. The arts flourished as well, particularly under the patronage of the powerful, and saintly, ruling Gonzaga family.

While today's visitors to beautiful Mantova may all rightly marvel at its rich array of history, architecture, art and culture, the Christian pilgrim gravitates to the Basilica of Sant' Andrea. In its crypt, the church houses the sacred relics of Christ's Precious Blood and of the holy martyr Saint Longinus, as well as the body of the fourth century Cappadocian Father of the Church, Saint Gregory Nazianzen. On every Good Friday, Mantova's sacred relics of Christ's Passion are brought out in a solemn procession for public veneration.

[ABOVE] View overlooking Mantova's Piazza Centrale.
[OVERLEAF] *Mantova: Piazza Centrale*, oil on canvas, 93 x 42 inches.

PADOVA

Santa Giustina Prayer

O LITTLE GIRL OF FAITH AND COURAGE, YOU GAVE YOUR LIFE TO UPHOLD YOUR BELIEF THAT JESUS IS LORD. I PRAY THAT THE LORD WILL LOOK KINDLY ON US WHO ARE WEAK AND NOT SO COURAGEOUS OR FAITHFUL. HELP US TO FIND A FAITH AS INNOCENT AND PURE AS THAT LITTLE CHILD'S.

[ABOVE] *Padova: Onion Domes*, watercolor, 30 x 22 inches.
[OPPOSITE] *Padova: Onion Domes on Santa Giustina*, oil on canvas, 40 x 46 inches.

WITH ALL DUE RESPECT TO DEAR SAINT ANTHONY, to whom Italians refer simply as *Il Santo* ("the Saint"), Padova—the city which houses Saint Anthony's world-renowned shrine and was the site of his preachings, teachings and burial—is far more than merely *la città del Santo* ("the city of the Saint.") For Padova is truly *la città dei santi* ("the city of saints"). As such, it's the destination of millions of pilgrims ever year.

Padova is hallowed with the presence of some of the most illustrious saints in Christendom. These holy men and women include apostles and evangelists, martyrs and confessors of the faith of Christ, as well as founders of local churches and religious communities. They ministered in Padova, they died in Padova, and they were venerated in Padova.

According to legend, Padova's origins trace far back in time to the year 1182 B.C., when it was supposedly founded by the survivors of the sack of Troy. Archaeologists have in fact found evidence that the Padova area was settled in the twelfth century B.C., but it is more likely that these earliest inhabitants came from the Veneto region, and were forerunners of the latter Venetians and not Trojan refugees. They came into contact with the Romans during the time of Rome's wars against Gaul and Carthage; by 49 B.C. they had formally become part of Roman Italy.

Evidence shows that Christianity grew firm roots in Padova early on. By A.D. 280 the Christian Church in Padova was already organized hierarchically, though the first documented reference to a particular local bishop is that of Crispin, who dates from the mid-300s. Saint Prosdocimus, a bishop and martyr, also dates to those earliest days: a mysterious and legendary figure, he is believed to be the founder of Padova's Christian Church.

One of the city's most revered and ancient saints is the martyr Saint Giustina (Justine), a victim of the anti-Christian persecutions instigated by the emperor Maximian. Following her martyrdom for the Faith, she was buried on October 7, 304, in a primitive Christian cemetery. A small martyr's shrine was erected over her grave, later replaced by a basilica. That church, in turn, was rebuilt in a more deserving manner in about A.D. 450 by the local ruler, Opilione.

Opilione also constructed the sacellum (oratory) of Saint Prosdocimus nearby, sometimes called the sacellum of Saint Mary. The oldest existing Christian oratory in Padova, it is now located—in nearly pristine condition—within the larger complex of the Basilica of Saint Giustina.

The Benedictine monks who arrived in Padova some centuries later built their monastery near the Basilica of Saint Giustina, and were charged with the spiritual care of the many pilgrims who came to venerate the saints honored there. These monks later came into possession of additional major relics when the bodily remains of Saint Luke the Evangelist and Saint Matthias the Apostle were brought from Constantinople by Saint Urius. Urius also brought a revered icon of the Madonna and Child, known as the Madonna of Constantinople, which was attributed in popular piety to the paintbrush of Saint Luke himself.

Saint Luke's bodily presence in Padova recently received major coverage in the international press when the Evangelist's tomb and remains underwent extensive forensic and archaeological studies. The studies support the authenticity of the relics, and the account of how they came to Padova. And they attract more pilgrims than ever to the Basilica of Saint Giustina.

Other relics came to Saint Giustina over the course of the centuries, including the purported remains of the Holy Innocents (the infants cruelly slaughtered by King Herod in Bethlehem), an early Christian martyr named Felicity, and the collected remains of numerous, nameless Christian martyrs from the Padova area. In addition, of course, are the remains of Saint Urius himself. The chapel

Padova: Blue Fountain, watercolor, 30 x 22¹/₄ inches.

of Saint Luke houses the tomb of Elena Lucrezia Cornaro Piscopia, a Benedictine Oblate who holds the great distinction of being the first woman in history to receive a University degree (from the University Padova in A.D. 1684).

Given this ancient and rich Christian history, why is Padova nevertheless so closely identified with Saint Anthony? Not only is Padova considered to be "the city of the Saint," but the Portuguese Anthony is known by all as "Anthony of Padova." But Anthony, born in Portugal, was not the first saint to live and die there by any means. Nor was he the first to attract huge crowds of pilgrims during his lifetime and after his death. He is not the only miracle-working saint in town, or necessarily the great-

est of Padova's many saints, given the exalted presence of apostles and evangelists in the same neighborhood. Perhaps his nearly universal popularity is derived as much from his endearing personal traits as from his extraordinary theological gifts.

Saint Anthony had the honor of receiving the unique title of "my bishop" or "theologian" from Saint Francis of Assisi. Francis, it is known, normally viewed formal education with a certain disregard, as offering the temptation to pride, and definitely working against poverty, since scholars needed books, and books were hand-written and bound at great expense. Such a life was not ideal for the mendicant friars who had taken vows of absolute

[LEFT] *Padova: The Prato*, oil on canvas, 59 x 49 inches.

[RIGHT] Donatello's equestrian statue outside the Basilica of Saint Anthony.

PADOVA: 7/11/99

The pilgrims coming to visit the shrine of Saint Anthony impress me. They are reflective and prayerful. Obviously they have come here for the sole purpose of praying at this shrine. "Il Santo," as Saint Anthony is called, is the focal point for the single most important pilgrimage in Italy.

The quiet piety one senses here is palpable. Outside stands a monumental equestrian statue; inside there is a crucifix of rare beauty. Both were made by Donatello, one of Italy's greatest sculptors. But throughout this basilica the pilgrim encounters wonderful art works that express the essential link between art and religion.

A recent visitor to Padova told his impressions upon entering the basilica and viewing the various art treasures in the church. He was struck by the faith and devotion of the many people kneeling there. At some point he remembered a friend who always goes to the saint when there is a major difficulty in her family. So he left the church, and began looking at postcards so he could write one to her. All of a sudden, as he relayed it, he was touched by the thought that he needed to return to the shrine and pray for his friend. Upon reentering and nearing Anthony's tomb he knelt and immediately set about praying. He felt touched by a feeling of peace, which is a hallmark of Saint Anthony. As he was about to leave, he heard a voice say: "And what about you?" He had forgotten to pray for himself. Huge tears began streaming down his face as the tremendous love and grace that he was being shown struck and overwhelmed him. Amen.

49

Blessed with love for the innocence and purity of children, your Saint Anthony showed a childlike innocence to all in his path. Help us to bring shelter, care, health, and joy to all in our path. Guide us to see in everything and everyone your loving concern.

poverty. Yet Francis made an exception for one exceptional friar, Anthony. For in Anthony, Francis recognized God's hand at work.

Though a great theologian and scholar, Anthony was graced with the common touch. He had the ability to translate sacred doctrine into sermons that were easily grasped by the great masses of the faithful who sought him out and followed him constantly. He was a sacred orator second to none, and passionately used his tremendous talent as a preacher to win back to the Church those who had been separated from her. But above all, Anthony was a man of tender compassion, who had infinite concern for the poor, the sick, the oppressed and those trapped by their own errors. It was not unusual for Anthony to win heretics back to the faith by means of simple stories and miraculous signs rather than clever theological arguments. During his lifetime and ministry, tale after tale was recounted of his miracles and loving concern for people. No wonder that these popular stories continued and multiplied exponentially after his death. As Il Santo had helped his beloved followers in life, he continued in death to intercede for them before the throne of God.

Thus Anthony's tomb became, and would remain, one of the most visited pilgrimage sites in all of Europe. The multi-domed, Byzantine-style basilica housing his sacred relics is a warm home to the faithful, who come to visit from all parts of the world. Tenderly caressing, kissing and embracing Anthony's stone tomb, which has been worn smooth from those same gestures repeated millions of times over the past eight centuries, the faithful pour out their needs to him in fervent prayer. And every year, those unable to visit him in person send to his basilica millions of letters requesting his powerful intercession, and thanking him for the favors granted them through his assistance.

Therein lies the secret of Anthony's popularity: a personal, loving connection to those in need, inspiring utter confidence and trust in those who seek him out. No mere "famous historical figure" or even an apostle or evangelist, Anthony is experienced personally as a friend, helper, consoler and miracle-working intercessor. The one known for working astonishing miracles in matters of great significance does not hesitate to assist a distracted day laborer who has lost his house keys, or an anxious mother whose child is running a fever. Like any real friend, he cares, and can always be counted on to help those in need. That is the secret of Saint Anthony of Padova's enormous popularity the world over.

[OPPOSITE] The Basilica of Saint Anthony in Padova.

GRADO &

WHAT A BEAUTIFUL STOP IN THIS PLACE TO VISIT OUR LADY OF THANKSGIVING. I LIFT UP MY HEART AND MY SOUL WITH EACH STOP TO THANK GOD FOR A MOTHER OF GRACE, FOR A MOTHER MOST CARING, FOR A MOTHER HIGHLY FAVORED IN HEAVEN AND ON EARTH. THANK YOU GOD, THE SUPREME MAKER OF ALL, FOR FAMILY, FOR FRIENDS, FOR LIFE. AMEN.

Grado: Leaning Tower, watercolor, 29 1/2 x 21 3/4 inches.

Aquileia, watercolor, 29⁷/₈ x 22¹/₈ inches.

Here on this site your faithful walked, sought shelter from war, fled to safety knowing you were always near. God, brighten our path with faith that you are with us. When our world seems to be threatened, to be ready to crumble and fall, give us the strength to continue walking in your dignity and your shelter. We ask this in the name. Amen.

AQUILEIA

A MINOR RAVENNA

TODAY, GRADO AND AQUILEIA ARE KNOWN more as a fashionable vacation destination—"The Sunny Isle between Venice and Trieste." But they formed a major religious center in the early centuries of Christianity. Located in Italy's northeastern Friuli-Venezia Giulia region, their locale offers pilgrims an unexpected concentration of sacred structures, riches and history found in few places outside of Rome, Milan, or Ravenna. One might even describe these two towns as a minor Ravenna.

Grado's history, in fact its very name, stems from its earliest days, and is inextricably intertwined with that of the larger, neighboring city of Aquileia to the north. *Gradus*—Latin for a step, rung or stop along the way to something else—aptly characterizes Grado's relationship to Aquileia. For many centuries, Grado was merely Aquileia's seaside stopover. The town would ultimately establish its own identity and importance when Aquileia was threatened by invasions from the Germanic tribes to the north. It would later find itself in a subordinate relationship to Venice, both politically and ecclesiastically.

Author Giuseppe Cuscito aptly describes the nature of this complex trio of associations:

> The history of Grado is interwoven with the history of Aquileia and of Venice; Grado shines between the twilight of Aquileia and the dawn of Venice; in that period—from the sixth to the tenth century—it lives a life of its own: before and after it lives a life that is merely reflected. Grado gathers the Roman inheritance of Aquileia, lovingly and fervidly cares for it over the course of various centuries, then hands it on to Venice. (*Grado e le sue basiliche paleocristiane, 6*)

A rich documentary history explains how Aquileia and Grado were originally settled. Celts from Gaul crossed the Alps and unwisely decided to settle in an area considered to be a strategic part of the Roman Empire. The squatters, regarded as a serious threat to Rome's national security, were quickly chased back over the Alps by a military expedition. In 181 B.C. Rome established a permanent presence of its own by founding the colony of Aquileia with an attached military garrison. By the reign of Augustus (27 B.C.–A.D. 14), Aquileia had a population of more than two hundred thousand, and was one of the greatest and most prosperous cities in the entire Roman Empire.

As it grew in size and importance, Aquileia became the periodic residence of imperial rulers, the seat of the governor of Italy's Tenth Region (Venetia-Hilaria), and headquarters for the commandant of the Upper Adriatic Fleet and the overseer of the State Mint. Throughout this time it served as a primary outpost against incursions of the northern barbarian tribes, and became a major staging point for military expeditions in the East.

The city later also became something of a staging point for Christian missionary excursions, and headquarters of the regional ecclesiastical structure. According to Aquileian Christian tradition, the Apostle Peter sent his young companion, the Evangelist Saint Mark, to preach the gospel in Rome's Tenth Region of Venetia-Hilaria: the capital of that region was Aquileia.

Saint Mark is said to have selected a certain Ermacora from among his many converts to serve as the leader of that new Christian community. Ermacora was taken to Rome by Mark, who introduced him to Saint Peter. The Apostle confirmed Mark's selection of Ermacora and appointed him the first bishop of Aquileia, thus sowing the seeds of the faith in the fertile soil of Aquileia and Grado.

While there is little archival evidence related to the earliest days of Christianity in Aquileia and Grado, there is abundant archaeological documentation that impressive buildings were already being erected for Christian

The Duomo Santa Eufemia was built in 579, and today it's surrounded by some lovely buildings dating from the Middle Ages. In this region I can smell the sea, and feel the cool salt water. Looking from the sea in the other direction I behold the marvel of hills, filled with vineyards that produce some of the best wines of Italy. God is especially provident here.

public worship in Aquileia during the early fourth century. And, as Aquileia's political and ecclesiastical influence expanded, ever-more-splendid and monumental constructions were built for both sectors. The city was continually visited by emperors and empresses, and hosted leading churchmen: Saints Athanasius, Jerome and Ambrose, among others. Its bishop received the rare and exalted title of Patriarch.

That patriarchal title and jurisdiction were later transferred to Grado. The transfer, and the actual physical relocation of the Aquileian population to Grado, were primarily due to the upheavals created by repeated early-fifth century invasions by the northern tribes, which endangered and disrupted the life of Aquileia far more than they did the isolated island of Grado. Grado also had a walled Roman military detachment, providing security for those seeking asylum. After Aquileia was substantially destroyed by Attila the Hun in A.D. 452, after undergoing a series of damaging raids in the first decade of the fifth century, the glory days of the city were over.

Visitors to the modern Grado and Aquileia are frequently astonished that those ancient, monumental buildings have survived relatively intact, and that many are still being used by the local faithful as centers of worship. Few are familiar with the cities' ancient histories, whether political or religious; fewer still seem aware of the artistic and architectural treasures preserved in these places.

Among the many Christian sites of particular interest to the pilgrim, Aquileia's cathedral church, the Patriarchal Basilica is of great significance. Dedicated some time after its construction to the Virgin Mary and the local church's founding saints Ermacora and Fortunato, the cathedral was begun by Bishop Theodore almost immediately after Emperor Constantine issued his "Edict of Milan" in A.D. 313. At that time, the emperor had an imperial residence at Aquileia. Even the most primitive structure erected by Theodore, shaped somewhat like a horseshoe, was of enormous size and proportions for that early period of religious tolerance. The complex of buildings was used for catechizing those interested in joining the Christian faith, for celebrating the rites of their Christian initiation like baptism and Chrismation, and for celebrating the Eucharist.

What visitors see today is basically the church as reconstructed and dedicated by the Patriarch Poppone in A.D. 1031. The structure is built upon only one of the three principal halls of the original church. A visitor entering the church will be struck by the remains of the original fourth-century mosaic floor, which measures thirty-seven by twenty meters. Like a great, multicolored carpet, it depicts symbolic representations of Christian doctrine and references to

Christ, the apostles and the Church. A crypt was excavated beneath the high altar in the ninth century to receive and protect the sacred relics of various local saints, including those of Saint Ermacora. It was decorated with fresco cycles of the life of Saint Mark the Evangelist, Ermacora and other saints involved in the presence of Christianity in Aquileia. To this day, all are still in good condition.

When the Crusaders returned to Europe from Palestine, they brought back stories of the sacred sites they visited. Since few Europeans would ever be able to personally visit the Holy Land and its shrines, many churches erected reconstructions—facsimiles—of those sacred places. Aquileia's cathedral contains such a shrine: it's a life-sized stone reproduction of the "Aedicule," the little building erected over Jesus' Tomb in Jerusalem's Church of the Holy Sepulchre, the site of Christ's burial and resurrection. The faithful unable to make a pilgrimage to Jerusalem could thus journey to Aquileia's cathedral to express their faith and devotion.

The basilica at the Paleo-Christian Museum site, outside Aquileia's city walls, is also significant. The unnamed Christian basilica dates to the early fifth century, and now houses—along with other buildings on the site—the museum, which features a rich display of notable Christian objects from the fourth through the ninth centuries. The sheer variety of art and architectural elements often elicits astonishment from museum visitors.

Grado boasts a number of magnificent religious structures, some of which date from before the transfer of the patriarchal dignity from besieged Aquileia. Most, however, are from the period of Grado's own patriarchal status. First among Grado's sacred edifices is its duomo, or cathedral, the Patriarchal Basilica of Santa Eufemia. This fifth-century structure, started by Bishop Niceta, was completed by the Patriarch Elias in the late sixth century. The building itself is sited on the remains of an even older church, dating from the late fourth century, that was built in the midst of a pre-Christian necropolis to serve the needs of Grado's growing Christian population. The basilica houses a number of rare treasures, including the church's famous

AQUILEIA: 7/15/99

After experiencing the crush of traffic near Venice (no amount of prayer could get anything to move!), we decided to head for the Friuli region, where there are ports, canals and the great ancient city of Aquileia. It may not be well known today, but in Jesus' time Aquileia was the second-largest port and twelfth-largest city in the empire, with a population of 250,000 when Attila the Hun attacked. The city was a great attraction at the time of the apostles. Some believe that Saint Mark the Evangelist was sent by Saint Peter to preach in the area, and founded the church here. I can't help but feel insignificant and small walking on the old stones along the same road once traveled by the ancients on their way to pray in their beautiful basilica. So much for all of my fretting over traffic, schedules and accommodations, which simply pales into insignificance.

Grado: 4th Century Church, watercolor, 30 x 21³/₄ inches.

fourteenth-century silver-gilt altar frontal, a plaster cast of the original sixth-century throne containing a relic of the true cross donated by Emperor Heraclitus, and the sacred relics of various local saints.

Bishop Niceta was also responsible for the Catholic Baptistery next to the duomo, which is remarkably well preserved. This octagonal structure is still equipped with its original, large hexagonal baptismal font made out of precious marble. For when Grado's military post saw an increasing presence of Arian Goths, this second baptistry was erected for their use.

Nearby is yet another jewel of Grado's ecclesiastical architecture: the church now known as Santa Maria delle Grazie. The earliest church on this site has been dated to the mid-fifth century, which suggests an intriguing origin to the church's current dedication. It may have been derived from the declaration at the Council of Ephesus, in A.D. 431, that the Blessed Virgin Mary should be rightly called "Mother of God." For soon after that doctrinal declaration, churches throughout Christendom hastened to dedicate churches to the honor and glory of the Blessed Virgin Mary, the Mother of God. (One of the more well-known examples is Rome's Saint Mary Major.) This is another indicator that Grado was hardly a Christian provincial backwater. In fact, regarding matters ecclesiastical, it was on the cutting edge.

Friuli: Orchard and Vines, watercolor, 28 x 20 inches.

UDINE

GATEWAY FROM THE EAST

Smack dab on the northern border of Slovenia and Italy I can see your Venetian windows, your glorious little piazzas. I see generations of children playing, calling, crying and praying. Here in this light of the Friuli region you ripen your harvest of grapes. People sip the new vintage. A joy abides as I walk through towards the southern regions. I can praise the Lord when it is beautiful. A spring of holy energy draws me on to give praise at the next station. Help me to praise when it is cloudy and dark. Help me to praise when it is dreary and cold.

If there is anything about Udine that the pilgrim traveler ought to understand, it would have to be the knowledge that the city lies on a major international route linking the southern and northeastern parts of Europe. Located in Italy's Friuli-Venezia Giulia region, far to the northeast, the city sits on the borders of Austria, Slovenia and the former Yugoslavia, also ensuring a link between the east and the west. The great international thoroughfare passing through the Friuli-Venezia Giulia region is like the European equivalent of the American Southwest's famous U.S. Route 66.

As travel-worn pilgrims know, a good road makes for an easy journey. Good roads actually tend to invite travelers to use them—to leave behind their familiar life at home, and to explore unknown places along the way. But sadly, there is no real control over which travelers choose to respond to the invitation of a good road. And there is no guarantee that those who take the journey will be welcome wherever the road takes them.

So is the situation of Udine and its surrounding regions. Over the millennia, the natural pass that cuts through the mountains dividing northern and southern Europe enabled large numbers of people to travel in both directions, for better or for worse. At times the movement was a migration, with one culture coming to another, resulting in the enrichment of both. Other times, though, the passage witnessed the movement of foreign military expeditions, which brought with them violence, illnesses, destruction and death on a grand scale. While a certain amount of "cultural exchange" inevitably took place under these conditions, it was usually at the point of a sword. Most often, the relationship was one of imposition and oppression.

Fairly constantly, and frequently, waves of religious, artistic, linguistic, musical and architectural influences have passed through this section of Italy, leaving significant traces in their wake. The process has taken place for centuries, and still continues unabated, dramatically so,

[ABOVE] *Udine: Palazzo Piazza*, watercolor,
17 x 13½ inches.
[RIGHT] *Udine: Palazzo Piazza*, oil on canvas,
60¼ x 42¼ inches.

even today. Interestingly, when one considers the current conflicts (and hopefully, dialogues) between East and West, Islam and Christianity, Orthodox Christianity and Roman Catholicism, one can have a credible hope for the future of Europe and the even broader world itself.

The area currently occupied by the city of Udine probably saw its first settlers as early as the second millennium B.C. Aside from archaeological evidence, documentation is sparse. The first mention made of the city in any existing document is in a charter dating from A.D. 983, in which the Holy Roman Emperor Otto II granted the castle of Udine and its resources to the patriarch of Aquileia.

An important turning point in Udine's "modern" history occurred in 1420, when the region became part of the Venetian Republic. For the next three-and-a-half centuries, the area was inseparably linked to the fate of Venice, as were the fates of so many regional population centers. As did Venice, the city went through Turkish raids, wars with the Holy Roman Emperor and the papacy in far-away Rome, and the like.

UDINE: 7/16/99

The road from Cividale and Grado winds through some of the most beautiful farmland I have ever seen. There are gentle hills, wonderful farms, and lush vineyards where the famous white wines of the Friuli region are born. I stop and paint along the way, and witness colors as sumptuous as the foods I've tasted.

In Udine there are several piazzas, with arcaded walkways and café chairs for locals and tourists to sit and quench their thirst. I stop under a large statue; facing me is a wonderful building with Venetian style arcades and small windows that scream out: "I'm worth a watercolor!" So I start working and discover some of the most interesting colors and shapes that I've painted yet. I don't know if it's the Byzantine influence of the architecture, or the light of Friuli that somehow got into my paint pots, but I love the effect of this town.

In 1797, Udine was occupied by Napoleon Bonaparte, but it fell by treaty to Austria in 1798. The French would remain regular visitors and occupiers, albeit on a sporadic basis. Only in 1813, with the post-Napoleonic future of Europe being settled, did the region officially receive the designation of Friuli, a name dating back to Imperial Roman times. The town participated with many others in the ill-fated, short-lived liberal republican uprising in 1848, and in 1866 was annexed to the kingdom of Italy. During World War I, Udine became headquarters for Italy's Supreme Command.

The site in the city that offers the most comprehensive view of the entire area, and a great story to boot, is the hill upon which Udine's castle is built. Local tradition purports that the spot only achieved its current elevation when it was built up by the troops of Attila the Hun. To provide their leader with a good observation platform, the soldiers used their helmets as pails to carry soil, thus raising the hill helmet-full by helmet-full. A gloating Attila watched from this newly constructed vantage point as noble Aquileia burned in the distance, another victim of Attila's raids.

The castle now occupying that hill has long served as the official residence of most of Udine's political and ecclesiastical rulers. In its current incarnation, construction dates from 1511. The castles built on that site were destroyed and resurrected many times, though not always as a result of military action. At least twice, the castle and other city structures were destroyed or seriously damaged by major earthquakes, in particular the massively destructive quake of 1511, and the more recent one of 1976. The castle shares occupancy of the hill with Udine's oldest still-standing church, the church of Santa Maria di Castello, which dates back to the Lombards. When the church was annexed to the larger church of Sant'Odorico in 1263, it lost its own parochial status.

Piazza della Libertá, located downhill from the castle and connected to it by a monumental Venetian Gothic portico and steps, is considered to be the very heart of the city. The piazza has been described as "the most beautiful Venetian square on the mainland," and rightly so. One can find within its confines and surroundings the very history of the city's rich and lengthy Venetian past, dating from 1420 through the late 1700s. Of particular note are the "Loggia del Lionello," with its alternating courses of pink and white stone (1448), the Renaissance "Loggia di San Giovanni" just opposite it across the piazza, the central fountain (1542), and the various columns and statues decorating the piazza.

A stroll along picturesque Via Mercatovecchio leads the visitor to the Piazza Matteoti-San Giacomo, the city's first square. Here are featured a number of outstanding monumental structures—among them, the central fountain (1543) designed by a pupil of Raphael, the ancient church of San Giacomo (1378), the town hall (a fascinating early-twentieth-century example of Art Nouveau), and the town's cathedral, dating in its current appearance from the 1300s. Near the cathedral are two masterpieces of the architectural skill of G. B. Tiepolo: his Purity Oratory (1757) and the Archbishop's Palace.

Pilgrims passing through this area should also visit the Sanctuary of Our Lady of Castelmonte, located about twelve miles east of the city, on the road passing through Cividale. The sanctuary is located so near Italy's border with both Austria and Slovenia that it's virtually an international destination. It is, in fact, the oldest Christian shrine in this part of Europe; it is counted among the oldest shrines of Christendom. And while its origins have been lost in time, there is documentary evidence that it existed in the fifth century. In fact, the Marian sanctuary of Castelmonte was already known before the Council of Ephesus (A.D. 431), which defined the dogma that the

Udine: Piazza della Libertá, pen and ink.

Blessed Virgin Mary, mother of Jesus Christ, is to be revered as *Theotokos*, the Greek theological term that translates to "Mother of God."

In the eighth century, Slavic people arrived in the area. Their earliest writings refer to the shrine of Castelmonte as the "Ancient Mountain," to Mary's image as "the ancient Madonna," and to nearby Cividale (once the Roman "Forum Julii") as "the Ancient Town." That they could do so in the 700s is yet another indication of Castelmonte's extremely early origins.

Documents from the years 1244–1247 speak of the glory of the shrine, calling it Santa Maria del Monte, and describe it in glowing terms as one of the most important and affluent of churches in the patriarchate of Aquileia. The crypt of the sanctuary's church is its most ancient part, and was originally the place where the image of the Madonna was revered. That image is locally referred to with exquisite tenderness as the "Madonna Bella." So lifelike is the statue that it is often called the "Madonna Viva."

How often I lose track of you, Lord, in my journey.
I lack the burning fervor of love that Lawrence knew.
Where have I been? What have I done?
Forgive my past and forgive my failings in the future.
Because it is that knowledge of your faithful caring for me
that lets me face my daily walk.

FROZEN IN TIME

RAVENNA & CLASSE

A beautiful mosaic of flowers
Birds in the trees, plants and deer
All creation is present in this mosaic
Which adorns a forlorn basilica.
Deserted by the sea, deserted by its people
This great artistic splendor of the sixth century
Still exists to smile on the passing pilgrim
And to open the eyes and hearts of those forlorn and feeling deserted.
Show us the greatness of your life in our world, Lord, that
We may praise and honor you and your world.

Classe: Sant' Apollinare, color marker.

SHORT OF INVENTING A FUNCTIONING TIME MACHINE to return to fifth-century Italy, there is literally nothing comparable to visiting the city of Ravenna on the Adriatic coast, to experience Roman ecclesiastical architecture in its most glorious embodiment. Not even Rome itself has the variety and extent of Ravenna's magnificent structures, which boast interior walls covered by unbroken expanses of luminous, multicolored mosaics. The ancient churches, basilicas, mausoleums and palaces of Ravenna and its nearby port city of Classe are unique in the Western world.

Those who happen upon these two unassuming towns, unaware of the unsurpassed ecclesiastical treasures that await them and unfamiliar with the towns' rich history, will be amazed to discover the marvels such relatively unknown places hold. In many ways, Ravenna and Classe are like their northern neighbors, Grado and Aquileia, hidden repositories of unimaginable Paleo-Christian relics.

But gaining a familiarity with the area's history will go a long way toward explaining why such marvels are found so out of the way. Over the course of various centuries, Ravenna went from being an insignificant settlement, haphazardly built on top of the sand dunes, to a major military base and Roman municipality. Simultaneously, its port of Classe developed into a major naval station of the Roman Empire.

Ultimately, Ravenna's importance derived both from its civil and religious significance. The city became the very capital of the Western Roman Empire itself, then served in a similar fashion as the capital of the northern warlords and kings who ruled over Italy after the deposition of the last Western Roman Emperor, Romulus Augustulus, in A.D. 476. Later, under the Eastern Roman Emperor Justinian, Ravenna became the seat of the Byzantine Empire's Prefecture of Italy,

and subsequently the headquarters of its resident military governors, the Exarchs.

Within Western ecclesiastical circles, Ravenna's Catholic bishop came to exercise a religious influence that periodically rivaled that of the Pope himself. It also had a profound missionary influence on Christianity in the Slavic countries beyond the far shores of the Adriatic Sea. Ravenna's better-known Catholic saints include Saint John Chysologus, Peter Damian and Saint Romuald. Ravenna was also the city of the divine poet Dante; his funeral and burial took place in the church of San Francesco in 1321.

Ironically, the presence of the Arian Gothic population in Ravenna is what explains the city's present-day collection of church-related treasures. The Arian version of Christianity, which denied the divinity of Christ, was condemned as heretical by the Church's earliest ecumenical councils: Nicea (A.D. 325) and Constantinople (A.D. 381). However this was an exceedingly popular and widespread heresy; for centuries it fluctuated between imperial support and imperial persecution.

The vast majority of the northern Gothic peoples who swept into Italy belonged to Arian Christianity, as did their rulers, who made generous provisions for the practice of their people's faith. Luckily they did so by establishing an Arian hierarchy alongside the existing Catholic hierarchy—erecting, on a grand scale, all the standard ecclesiastical buildings required for a local church, such as the bishop's cathedral with its contiguous baptistery, and a palace for the bishop and his officials.

Today's visitors to Ravenna can be doubly grateful: first, that the Arian Gothic rulers felt themselves under no compulsion to destroy their Catholic opponents' churches, but simply created an Arian church structure that paralleled and duplicated the preexisting Catholic organization. Second, that the Catholics, in turn, opted not to destroy the Arian structures when Catholicism prevailed as the dominant form of Christianity in Ravenna. Rather than destroy the Arian heretics' buildings, the Catholics cleverly rededicated them to their own purposes and saints. And so both Catholic and Arian structures were saved for posterity, much to the delight of those who now visit the sites.

Confronted with this veritable "embarrassment of ecclesiastical riches," a visitor to Ravenna and Classe needs to be selective and seek out structures of particular religious, cultural and historical significance.

Of the Catholic structures, there's the edifice traditionally designated the "Mausoleum of Empress Galla Placidia" (who died in A.D. 450), which was more likely built as an oratory dedicated to the honor and glory of the popular Roman martyr Lawrence. Once connected to the Palatine (Imperial) Chapel of Santa Croce, the mausoleum is considered by experts to have the oldest, most complete and most beautifully decorated mosaic interior in Ravenna, a city known for its extraordinary mosaics. The interior's otherworldly splendor of lapis blue vaulting, studded with golden stars and the glorious, triumphant Cross, seems intended as a foretaste of heaven itself, and stands in sharp contrast with the diminutive building's rough brick exterior.

Often overlooked among the flashier sites of Ravenna is a little gem of a church called the Imperial Basilica of San Giovanni Evangelista. This is the oldest church in Ravenna, constructed in A.D. 426 by Empress Galla Placidia, in fulfillment of a sacred vow she made under perilous circumstances. While on a voyage from Constantinople to Ravenna to rule the Western Empire as Regent for her son, five-year-old Emperor Valentinian III, her ship was caught in a violent storm off the coast of Ephesus in modern-day Turkey. The empress turned toward the city revered as the final dwelling place of the Blessed Virgin Mary and of John

the Evangelist, Jesus' Beloved Disciple, and desperately prayed to Saint John. She solemnly swore that if she and the imperial family were spared from death at sea, she would erect a votive church in his honor. Popular piety holds that the empress' prayer was answered immediately when Saint John himself appeared, took the helm, and steered the storm-tossed ship into calmer waters. From there the ship continued its voyage and arrived safely in Ravenna, and news of the miraculous event spread throughout the Empire. Faithful to her vow, the empress began construction of the votive church. She had both the arch and the dome of the church's apse decorated with mosaic portraits of the imperial family, as well as a representation of John the Evangelist miraculously saving the empress and her children from the tempest at sea.

Over the centuries the church would suffer from both natural disasters and unfortunate structural modifications. Though it was restored to its pristine condition in the early 1900s, it suffered severe damage during two Allied bombing raids in 1944. Restored yet again, the basilica now closely reflects the simplicity of the original restoration. San Giovanni Evangelista is a touching, personal link to members of the imperial family, and a memorial to a real-life event that almost changed the course of Western history as we know it.

The Catholic cathedral or duomo was originally dedicated under the title of "Hagia Anastasis" (Holy Resurrection) and built by Bishop Ursus in the early fifth century after Emperor Honorius transferred his Western Imperial Capital to Ravenna from Milan. A city raised to the rank of Imperial Capital had need of its own bishop and cathedral, the bishop's church. Even a cursory glance at the duomo by a first-time visitor will reveal that the church has been rebuilt a number of times—most recently in the eighteenth century. Nothing of the church's ancient origins is visible other than its most famous accoutrement, the sixth-

Ravenna, watercolor, 30 x 22¹/₈ inches.

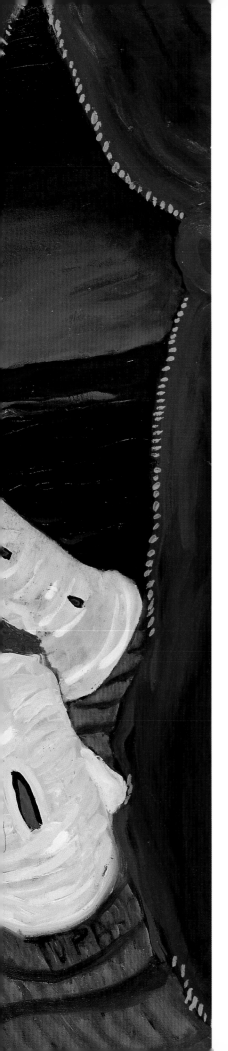

CLASSE: 7/19/99

Sunrise at Sant' Apollinare. The birds start singing. By the entryway is a beautiful white pigeon that looks like it could have come from one of the mosaics in this fifth-century basilica. I sense the pigeon is part of the landscape imagined by a great artist fifteen hundred years ago who has departed without leaving his name. It is peaceful here today, yet in the history of this city and its churches filled with such beauty there is also another reality. For these were the scenes of bloody battles. Totilla, chief of the Lombards, fought and captured this city for a time. The heresy of Arianism and Montanism was stamped out here with the killing of any known adherents.

It is always amazing to me how great beauty can be created in the midst of utter barbaric violence. I find that painting around this building is a slow learning process, as the church seems so simple, yet it eludes me. While drawing in San Vitale I was enjoying the colors and relentless painted stare of the emperor and his wife, when a woman of a certain age knelt before the altar and reminded me of the meaning behind the great churches of Emperor Justinian. All of the great art and architecture is simply there to help us kneel in awe and wonder at the genius of God's creation. The figures of Theodora and Justinian somehow embody, then, the essence of eternal watchfulness.

[LEFT] *Ravenna: Theodora meets Classe*, oil on canvas, 59 x 49 inches.

Classe: Facade, watercolor, 29⁷/₈ x 22¹/₄ inches.

century pulpit of Bishop Agnello. One of its altars contains the sacred relics of Bishops Esuperantius and Maximian; another has those of Saint Barbatianus.

Part of the cathedral complex is found next door to the duomo, the cathedral baptistery ("Battisterio Neoniano," or "Degli Ortodossi"). While the beautiful octagonal font itself dates from the fourth century, Bishop Ursus erected the building in the early fifth century, at the same time as he constructed his cathedral. Still existent are mosaics dating from around A.D. 450, commissioned by Bishop Neone. And the church's interior contains four small apses, a fairly rare architectural element.

The Archiepiscopal Palace, also part of the complex, now houses a major museum, featuring a group of precious mosaics that decorate the palace chapel. Erected by a certain Archbishop Peter, the chapel once contained the silver "Agnello cross"—dating from A.D. 557—that is now itself displayed in the museum. Also displayed is the famous carved ivory throne of Archbishop Maximian, dating from the early sixth century. Impressive for its richly carved surfaces, the throne was possibly donated to the Archbishop by the Emperor Justinian himself.

Of the Arian structures in Ravenna, there is also a great trove. Shortly after conquering Ravenna in A.D. 493,

King Theodoric embarked on a building campaign to provide churches for his Arian Gothic people. One of these was the Arian cathedral, later "reconciled" or reconsecrated as a Catholic church in A.D. 561 under the title of San Teodoro, and now known as the church of Spirito Santo. Its nearby octagonal baptistery, also built by Theodoric, was later reconciled as the Catholic church of Santa Maria around A.D. 555. Like its Catholic counterpart, the Arian baptistery also has four small apses.

Theodoric built the Basilica of Sant' Apollinare Nuovo (493–526) as an Arian church dedicated to the Savior. Under the patronage of Saint Martin of Tours, known as the *Malleus Haereticorum* ("Hammer of Heretics"), the church was reconciled to the Catholic community around A.D. 555. When, in the middle of the ninth century, the sacred relics of Saint Apollinarius were solemnly brought to the church from their unprotected resting place in the basilica at Classe, the name of the church was changed to Sant' Apollinare Nuovo ("new" Sant' Apollinare.) While most famous for the stunning mosaics that run the length of the nave's side walls (which mainly go back to the time of Theodoric), the church also houses a marvelous fifth- and sixth-century marble pulpit, altar, chancel screen and throne.

Born of multiple parentage, the church of San Vitale was begun by the Arian Goths under Bishop Ecclesius in A.D. 527. Twenty years later, it was finished and consecrated by Byzantine Catholics under Archbishop Maximian. (A.D. 547 was the year Saint Benedict died at Monte Cassino, to put this church in a Western historical context.) San Vitale is built on an octagonal plan, with a narthex at the main entrance and an apse with two small chapels in the sanctuary area—so typical of Byzantine church architecture. The nave is nearly surrounded with a multileveled series of galleries for viewing the liturgy, including a rare *matroneum* ("women's gallery"), from the time when women were excluded from the body of the church and kept separate from the men. Some of the finest mosaics in all of Christendom are concentrated in the choir and apse areas of this church, including the world-famous portraits of Emperor Justinian and his wife, Empress Theodora.

Though not located in the city center, the Mausoleum of King Theodoric (who died in A.D. 526) is well worth the one-mile trip to the Gothic burial area. An architectural oddity, Theodoric's last resting place is a two-layered stone structure roofed with a single, enormous carved stone that measures thirty-six feet in diameter and ten feet in height. The king's stone sarcophagus is located in the building's upper level.

One must also make sure to journey to the ancient sea port of Classe, which lies outside of Ravenna on dry land that was once the Adriatic coast. Apparently, Classe's castrum (military camp) was the area's first Christian settlement, and it was to the merchants and seamen of the castrum that the pioneering bishop of Ravenna, Apollinarius, first preached. The church dedicated to him, the Basilica of Sant' Apollinare in Classe, was started by Bishop Ursicinus in A.D. 525 next to the early Christian cemetery where Saint Apollinarius was buried. Completed and consecrated in A.D. 549 by Bishop Maximian, it received the addition of a bell tower some five hundred years later. As at San Vitale, the extraordinarily brilliant mosaics of this church are located in the arch and apse dome, which depicts the blessed bishop standing in lush, heavenly fields amidst the sheep that represent his flock. The church itself is virtually the only vestige of ancient Classe still visible to a casual visitor. But for the truly determined aficionado, there are archaeological excavations located at the site of the old sea port, some distance away.

SANT' AGATA FELTRIA

THE LOST VILLAGE

God gives treats!

Lord, these builders wanted to touch your sky.

This lost little village shows me that people can live in beauty and wonder.

Thank you for our simple back roads! Thank you for the olive groves! Thank you for architects that open our eyes and hearts! Yes, we have a treat here.

I want to sing Your praise and thanksgiving for artistic talent and for a part in your creation.

The few people who purposely seek out the little town (of around three thousand inhabitants) of Sant' Agata Feltria in Le Marche, near the borders of Toscana and of Emilia Romagna, are—more than likely—the devoted fans of this area's rare white truffles. Each year, in mid-October, the truffle lovers gladly make the long and difficult journey to Sant' Agata, to join in the town's annual celebration of its famous *tartufo bianco*.

Sant' Agata Feltria—formerly known as Pietra Anellaria—has its origins in the pre-Etruscan times of the local Umbran people. It then passed through the usual historical succession of inhabitants: Umbrans, Etruscans, Romans, northern Germanic tribes, Byzantines, Longobards and the constantly warring local noble families of feudal and then Renaissance times. The entire region, as well as the town itself, was fought over for cen-

Sant' Agata Feltria, watercolor, 29¹³/₁₆ x 22¹/₈ inches.

turies. The castle-fortress atop the hill was initially built in the tenth century by Raniero Cavalca, and over the course of the following centuries saw improvements and expansion. The hill rising above the town, Monte Ercole (or Mount Hercules) has been known since Roman times for its luxuriant chestnut forest. This combination—a hill named after a pagan god, and an ancient grove of chestnut trees—leads to the conclusion that this is a site long considered sacred to the inhabitants of this settlement.

A major note of historical importance needs to be stressed regarding this part of Italy, this corner of the country where Le Marche, Toscana and Emilia Romagna come together. This region was the scene of constant warring among the great local feudal families. The Malatestas,

Driving through the heart of the Marche region of Italy, I am feeling sick from the twists and turns of country roads. Tiny little lanes that wend their way up and around the mountains. Beautiful trees, lush mountain fields of sunflowers, and ever present flocks of sheep and herds of cattle. Then, after taking a bend in the road, all of a sudden there's a marvelous sight: Across a sea of olive trees is a town crowned with castles and towers. It is indeed a picture postcard. When I looked at the map there wasn't even a dot! I can't resist exploring this beautiful lost village.

Montefeltros, della Roveres, Sforzas and Fregosos all battled for control of this rich area. In the regional political conflicts, capturing a small, fortified town like Santa' Agata Feltria made the difference between being a minor lord and a major player. But those same warlords also provided the artistic patronage that gave the town's palaces and churches their rich trove of paintings and sculptures. Duke Federico of Montefeltro, for example, built the palazzo now housing the municipal government, and ordered that the old Rocca be enlarged and beautified by Francesco di Giorgio Martini in 1474. The two polygonal bastions seen today are the result of that particular project. At that point the castle came to be called the Rocca Fregoso, for the family name of Federico of Montefeltro's son-in-law. The town currently uses the Rocca Fregoso as a museum, and it's also a stunningly dramatic venue for performances.

The town's historic center and most of its medieval walls and buildings remain unchanged today, offering the visitor a rare opportunity, in an uncrowded setting, to explore what a medieval town actually looked like. Among Sant' Agata Feltria's most interesting highlights are the sixteenth-century church of San Girolamo, built by the Fregoso family; the seventeenth-century church of San Francesco, featuring an acclaimed carved marble holy water font that dates from 1532; and the Convent of the Poor Clares, housing a major collection of rare parchments from the twelfth through fourteenth centuries. Other treasures of the town include the tenth-century Collegiate Church, the Convent of San Girolamo, the church of Nostra Signora delle Grazie, and the church of Sant' Apollinare, which houses a miraculous image of the Blessed Virgin Mary. Lest the pilgrim think there is only one spiritual draw to Sant' Agata, it must be pointed out that the sixteenth-century church of the Cappuchin Friars boasts its own miraculous image, the Madonna dei Cappuchini.

[OPPOSITE] *Sant' Agata Feltria: The Castles*, oil on canvas, 59 x 49 inches.

Urbania: Sunflowers, watercolor, 29⁷/₈ x 22¹/₄ inches.

Urbania: Parco Ducal, watercolor, 30 x 22¹/₄ inches.

PILGRIMS ON THE ROAD TO ROME have the opportunity to visit many alternative pilgrimage sites: Assisi, Bobbio, Loreto, Montecassino, Padova and Subiaco are among the better-known. But there are also any number of lesser-known places, each having its own religious significance and natural beauty. Urbania, nestled in the hills of Italy's northeastern Le Marche region, is one such place. Originally known as Castel delle Ripe, Urbania was a Free Commune protected by its community of Benedictine monks. In 1282 it was renamed Castel Durante, and during the late Middle Ages and the Renaissance was synonymous with the production of exquisite polychrome majolica ceramics (an art still practiced there). A number of the most renowned families of ceramists in Europe plied their art there. The town fell under the control of various local families who built its massive defensive walls; from 1424–1631 it was ruled by the Montefeltro and Della Rovere families, after which it entered into the Papal States and was renamed Urbania in honor of the reigning pontiff, Pope Urban VIII. The town's great Benedictine abbey was suppressed and became a diocese, its abbey church was transformed into the cathedral, and its monastery was turned into the bishop's palace in 1636.

Urbania, itself the birthplace of the renowned Renaissance architect Bramante, lies only a few kilometers away from Urbino, often described as "the ideal Renaissance city." It is the birthplace of artist-architect Raphael and political center of the famed Renaissance patron of the arts, Duke Federico di Montefeltro. The two locations are intimately connected: Urbania, which formed part of the Duchy of Urbino, was the site of one of the Duke's principal palaces and favorite hunting lodge. But Urbania's history and significance long predate the Duke's fifteenth-century renown.

"To speak of Urbania is to speak also of Saint Christopher," said the late Don Ugo Donato Bianchi, who was Archbishop of Urbino, Urbania and Sant' Angelo in

YOU AMONG ALL WOMEN, AMONG ALL CHILDREN, KNOW OUR NEEDINESS. YOU KNOW OUR WEAKNESS, YOU KNOW OUR INNOCENCE. INTERCEDE FOR US THAT WE MAY SEE OUR WORLD WITH THE EYES OF WONDER. PROTECT US AS WE WALK, AS WE SLEEP. PROTECT US AGAINST ALL OF OUR FOES, AGAINST ANY EVIL THAT MAY BE IN OUR WAY. WE MAKE THIS PRAYER THROUGH YOU TO JESUS OUR LORD IN THE SPIRIT TO THE MAKER OF ALL.

URBANIA

THE HOLY BABY

Vado. He could just as well have said, "To speak of Urbania is to speak also of Saint Benedict," for both saints are closely connected with Urbania's history.

First, Saint Benedict: The Patron of Europe and father of Western Monasticism was born in Nursia, Umbria, in the late fifth century A.D. He died in Montecassino in the mid-sixth century. Local tradition recounts Saint Benedict himself visiting the area that is now Urbania on one of his rare journeys away from his monastery, but at any rate it is clear that by the seventh century there was already a major foundation of Benedictine monks there. They built a monastery and monastic church on the ruins of a Roman temple dedicated to Hercules, and dedicated their foundation to Saint Christopher under the title San Cristoforo del Ponte (Saint Christopher of the Bridge). The name refers to the Roman bridge over the Metauro river that gave access to the town, as well as to Saint Christopher, who once lived on a riverbank. When Benedictine nuns arrived in the area later (probably in the twelfth century), they established their monastery on the far side of the Metauro.

The life of Saint Christopher is shrouded in mystery. His feast day was actually removed from the Roman Calendar of Saints in the 1960s, and devotion to him is therefore less universal than it once was. Yet his story is a fascinating one, containing kernels of historical information among its symbolic elements. What is known is that Christopher was a Christian martyr of Lycia who died in the persecutions of A.D. 250. He was a Roman soldier and Christian convert; in his deep fervor he engaged far too publicly (for the times) in preaching the religion of Christ to his fellow soldiers. Refusing to renounce his newfound faith in Christ, he suffered a number of horrible tortures and was finally beheaded. He was venerated early on by the Church, first in the East and then in the West, especially in Austria, Dalmatia, Spain and Italy.

But if those early stories of Christopher's life offered little in the way of detail, the thirteenth-century "Golden Legend" of Jacopo da Voragine made up for that. The work, with its richly embroidered narratives and moral lessons, was truly responsible for popularizing the saint in the West. The story it recounts involves a man called Reparatus, who was of heroic stature and spent his life seeking someone to serve. He ultimately came to hear of Christ, the one person truly worth serving, and sought conversion to Christianity. A holy hermit instructed him for his baptism.

In preparation for the sacrament, Reparatus practiced charity to his fellow men and women. Given his extraordinary size and strength, he assisted travelers crossing a local river that had no bridge, carrying them on his broad shoulders. But on one particularly stormy night, when the river was swollen from the rain and the currents wilder than ever, Reparatus was asked to ferry a young boy. Leaning on his great staff, the giant man was barely able to cross the roiling waters. All the while, the child seemed to be getting heavier and heavier.

Finally Reparatus reached the river's far bank. And the child explained that he was, in fact, Jesus Christ, the one whom Reparatus had long been seeking. The heaviness that Reparatus had felt was the weight of the world's sins which Jesus bore out of love for humanity, a weight that Reparatus had helped Christ to bear during the crossing. Reparatus was then baptized, receiving the descriptive name of Christopher—Greek for "Christbearer." He is still frequently depicted holding his tree-sized staff, which later miraculously blossomed and took root. Appropriately he became the patron saint of travelers, drivers, tourists, letter-carriers and athletes; due to his flowering staff, he is also the patron saint of fruit-vendors. And he is one of the fourteen famous "Auxiliary Saints" that Christians invoke in times of special need.

To the Benedictines, it made sense to dedicate their church and home to Christopher: the buildings sat on the site of an ancient pagan temple dedicated to the Hellenic hero, Hercules, and Christopher is, in all his strength, a kind of Christian Hercules. Also, the town was surrounded on three sides by the Metauro river, recalling the legendary river of Christopher's story. In time, Saint Christopher became the patron of the town as well, and then the entire diocese.

Urbania's cathedral houses a shrine to the saint that contains a major relic, purported to be a bone from the saint's shoulder upon which Jesus sat during the crossing. Held in a marvelously wrought silver urn by Antonio Pollaiuolo, the relic was presented to the town in 1472 by Cardinal Giovanni Bessarion, Patriarch of Constantinople and Abbot Commendam of the monastery of Saint Christopher, in the presence of Duke Federico da Montefeltro. The cathedral also has a beautiful eighteenth-century polychrome wooden statue of the saint. And each year, on July 25, Saint Christopher is celebrated with great festivity: there is a solemn Eucharist, followed by processions and the blessing of townspeople and motorists with the relic of their patron saint.

The Benedictine nuns who took up residence on the far banks of the Metauro river, probably in the twelfth century, have contributed their own miraculous image, equally revered by Urbania's faithful. This is the image of the Blessed Virgin Mary housed in the Benedictine women's monastery of Santa Maria Maddelena. In the 1700s, the community of nuns was presented with the image of Mary as a young baby, dressed in swaddling clothes. It was sent by the Franciscan mystic, Saint Veronica Giuliani, and brought in a wicker basket to the monastery by an old man who mysteriously disappeared from sight. Pinned to the image was a handwritten note (purporting to be the words Mary herself had spoken to Saint Veronica on behalf of the Benedictines) promising special blessings to that community of nuns if they would honor her as their special patron, and prayerfully invoke her aid in their times of need.

The nuns and the townspeople have done just that. Since the 1700s, devotion to *la Santa Bambina* has been one of the major hallmarks of religious life and practice in Urbania. The monastery's ancient chronicles list miracle after miracle attributed to the Santa Bambina's intercession, including a contemporary miracle. It took place during World War II when, in June 1944, Allied bombers mistakenly dropped their excess tonnage on Urbania, killing hundreds of people as they emerged from the cathedral's Sunday morning High Mass. But although bombs fell all around the monastery perimeter, none fell within the walls, or did any damage to the nuns who were on their knees in prayer before their beloved Bambina.

On Santa Bambina's feast day, September 8, all the town's children bring flowers, songs and prayers to the Madonna in the chapel of the nuns' monastery. On that date in 1988, a rare event took place: to mark the close of the Marian Year, the image left the cloistered nuns' church for the first time. The Santa Bambina was brought through the torch-lit, gaily decorated streets to the cathedral, and then carried on a silk cushion in the arms of a young priest at the front of a great procession of the archbishop, his clergy, townspeople, and faithful who came from miles away. She was received at the cathedral church, the former Benedictine Abbey of Saint Christopher, with bells ringing and handkerchiefs waving in greeting. A solemn High Mass and the Litany of the Blessed Virgin Mary, the Litany of Loreto, were sung in the presence of the venerated image before it was returned in procession to its home in the Benedictine nuns' monastery.

LORETO

HOME OF THE HOLY HOUSE

I really feel powerless in our world. Like many people, I am afraid of families disappearing or seeming weaker. How do we strengthen the bonds of love in our world? How do we strengthen faith, hope and love? In this house of the holy family, make all families holier, more loving and more joyful!

Blessed family of Palestine, Jewish family chosen by God, bring peace to the homes of your land. Bring them comfort, shelter, warmth and love. Blessed family of Nazareth, in a world occupied by foreign legions you brought the light of faith, truth and justice. Let your peoples living in your land find the same. Help the war weary, help the war angry, help peace find a home.

This is how the world famous—and controversial—shrine in Loreto is described by Pope John Paul II: "The Holy House of Loreto is the first sanctuary of international importance dedicated to the Virgin and is the true Marian heart of Christianity."

Loreto, a medieval hill town in Italy's Le Marche province, has been the goal of millions of devout pilgrims, both Christian and Muslim. For centuries they have journeyed here, drawn by the town's bold claim that it contains within its borders the very stone walls that once sheltered the Holy Family of Nazareth: Jesus, Mary and Joseph.

Even more astonishing, the stones of the Holy House's walls are said to have been transported to this corner of Italy, from Galilee itself, "by angelic ministry!" The most familiar description says that the conveyance happened by air. This has produced celebrated stories and images of the flying house, borne on the shoulders of angels, with the Madonna and Child riding the ridge line of the roof. It also explains why the Catholic Church has chosen the Madonna of Loreto as the patroness of pilots, passengers and aviation in general.

Two less familiar accounts of the house's angelic translation has it taking place by sea. In one, the house plows its way through the waves, borne up by angels immersed in the waters, with the Madonna and Child riding safely on the roof above. In the other account, the house's individ-

Loreto: Piazza, watercolor, 30 x 22¼ inches.

ual stones are transported in a pile on the deck of a sailing vessel accompanied by angels, while the Madonna and Child look benignly upon the scene from the sky above.

Recent literary and archaeological investigations have brought to light the actual origins of what many had simply dismissed as a pious tale. These same investigations have also affirmed the wisdom that even the seemingly wildest story usually contains at least a kernel of truth and historicity. In Loreto's case, scholars recently discovered a document dating from September 1294, that details the gifts that Niceforus Angeli ("Angels"), ruler of Epirus, bestowed upon his daughter Ithamar on the occasion of her wedding to Philip of Taranto. Among the gifts described are "the sacred stones carried away from the House of Our Lady, the Virgin Mother of God."

That literary evidence supports the explanation that the "sacred stones" come from the House of the Virgin in Nazareth. They were most likely removed from the church of the Annunciation there sometime during the Crusader period, and transported to Italy—by sea—at the direction of the head of the Angeli family (in other words, by the "angels"). There, the stones became part of Ithamar's dowry.

Archaeology and graphic studies alike point to Galilee as the origin of the Holy House's stones. Geologically, this type of stone is found in the area of Nazareth; the tech-

Route to Loreto, watercolor, 29⁷/₁₆ x 21⁷/₈ inches.

Hills Near Loreto, watercolor, 29⁷/₈ x 22¹/₄ inches.

[LEFT] *Loreto: The Holy House*, pen and ink.
[OPPOSITE] *Loreto: The Holy House*, oil on canvas, 59 x 48 inches.

niques and manner in which these stones were shaped correspond to the techniques used in first-century Galilee, and match the stones still remaining in the church of the Annunciation. Graffiti scratched into some of the house's stones by pilgrims are attributable to Jewish Christians, and are similar to graffiti that was found in Nazareth.

But even without the benefit of modern science, seven hundred years of faithful pilgrims have recognized in the Holy House of Loreto a sacred relic directly linked to the Holy Family of Nazareth. So the pilgrims arrive by the millions, many with enormous difficulty, to venerate the place where the Virgin dwelt, for in this place, the Virgin said "Yes" to God's plan to save humanity. This is where the Incarnation took place and where the "Word became flesh." This is where the Holy Family dwelt in love, where Joseph taught Jesus the carpenter's trade, where Joseph aged, grew sick and died in the loving presence of Jesus and Mary, and where Jesus bid good-bye to his mother and left to fulfill his divine mission.

These sacred, humble walls of stone, though encased since 1507 in precious carved marble panels designed by Bramante and housed within a cavernous Renaissance-era basilica, are still considered "home" for the followers of Jesus and for those who love the Blessed Virgin Mary. To cite one of Pope John Paul II's *Angelus* discourses:

> Loreto is a place of peace for the soul, of personal encounter with God; it is a refuge for those who seek Truth and the meaning of their lives. Loreto is the Sanctuary of the Incarnation, which proclaims the love of God, the dignity of each person, the holiness of the family, the value of labor and of silence, the necessity of prayer, the commandment of love toward all our brothers and sisters.

LORETO: 7/24/99

My memory of this place is of a very beautiful setting with streams of people walking past as I am kneeling. I think of the families with their avid and intense stares as they approach the shrine, hoping to find a deeper insight into their faith, or a mystery that will reconnect them to that great, pure direct light that is God. I sense a special grace or even visible faith in their movement. What a wonder we are as people. We hear about something greater than ourselves, we perhaps intuit it, we search to glimpse it, yet we are always trying to touch it. Going to a special place and touching the stones that perhaps Mary mother of God saw or touched becomes a place where I can then be closer to God, to Mary, and to the mystery of love.

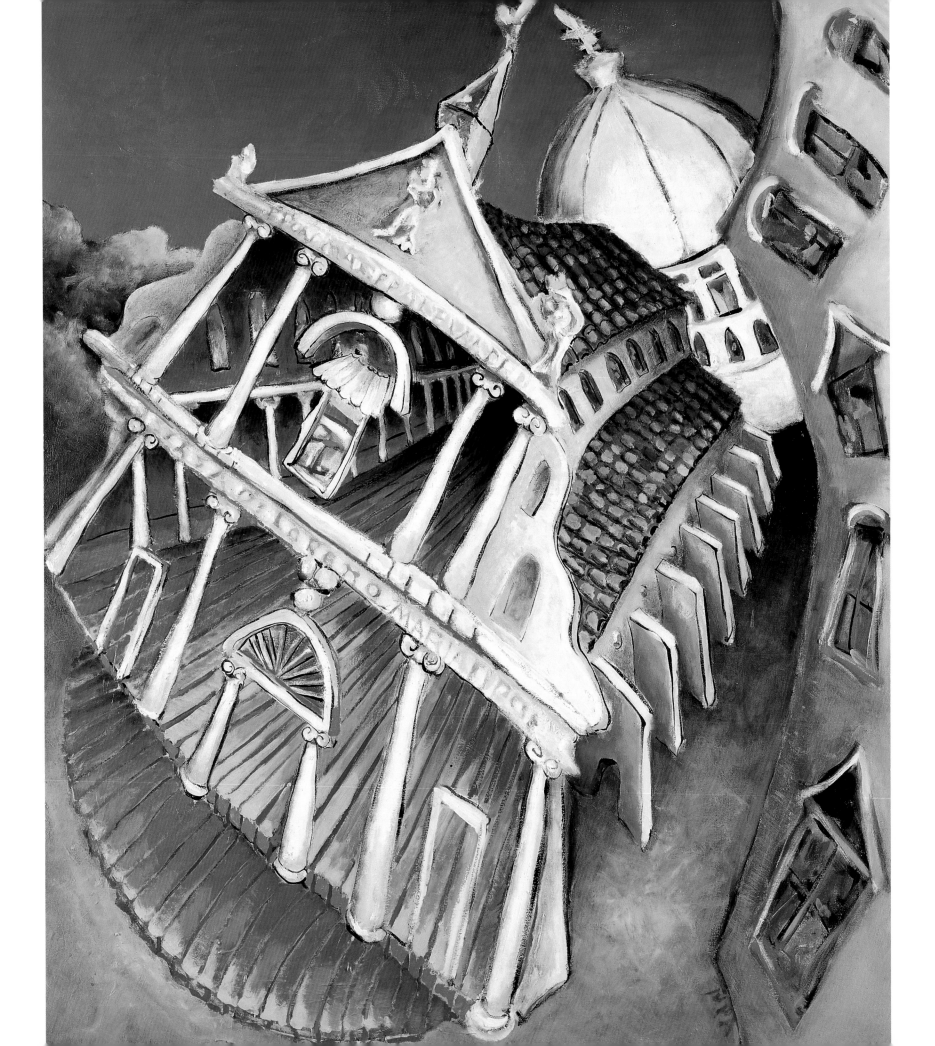

GUBBIO

Saint Ubaldo, a great diplomat, used his inner voice of strength to stop an advancing army. A wolf stopped saint Francis with a great roar and was loved into friendship and peace. Lord how great are your signs and wonders. How can I understand? What is to stop me from being wholly absorbed in You? Give me the strength to speak and the love to tame.

WHERE FRANCIS TAMED THE WOLF

The name of Gubbio may ring a bell for anyone familiar with the life of Saint Francis of Assisi, for it was in Gubbio that he tamed the ferocious, man-eating wolf. But long before Francis of Assisi had ever set foot in Gubbio, or accomplished this wondrous, unforgettable feat, Gubbio already had a venerable history. Like so many of Umbria's local hill towns, it traces its origins back to Etruscan times. Its subsequent Roman phase was significant enough that among its ruins is an almost perfectly preserved Roman amphitheatre, which sits outside the present city walls.

In Christian times, the people of Gubbio came to honor its medieval bishop, Saint Ubaldo, as its savior—in A.D. 1155, Ubaldo himself persuaded the Emperor Frederick Barbarossa to spare the city from destruction. Saint Ubaldo's feast day, May 15, is still celebrated annually by the entire town, and the festival rites are known throughout all of Italy. The holiday is the setting for the famous race of the ceri, in which three wax statues of the town's patron saints, each mounted on a heavy wooden tower, are carried on the shoulders of local youths from the

[ABOVE] *Gubbio*, pen and ink.

86

town's various districts. The groups compete against each other, carrying their neighborhood saint's image, as they race to the top of the mountain where the monastery of Sant' Ubaldo stands.

Soon after Francis of Assisi, born Francesco di Bernardone, so dramatically stripped himself naked in the courtyard of the Bishop's Palace, the young man left Assisi dressed in the simple garb he was given by one of the bishop's servants. He had no idea where he was going, and was simply committed to doing God's will, whatever that might prove to be. On the road toward his unknown future he was set upon by bandits, who beat him mercilessly when they discovered he had nothing worth stealing—and that he was even poorer than they were.

The bruised traveler continued on his journey, following the road to the Benedictine Abbey of San Verecondo located outside the town of Gubbio. There, among the monks, Francis sought refuge and recuperation. Soon, he began to work as a domestic servant, but quickly realized it was not his calling. He left the monastery and went into Gubbio, seeking out lodgings from a friend. This friend, one Federico Spadalunga, gave Francis a change of clothes—a simple tunic to replace what the bishop's servant had donated. That tunic would become inextricably associated with Saint Francis. It would come to be known as the Franciscan habit, worn by all his followers.

While Francis was in Gubbio, he heard from terrified citizens that a ravenous wolf was prowling the town. Not only did it attack and eat their livestock, it did something far more shocking. It killed humans as well.

Francis, however, was not terrified. He astounded his hosts by striding, unescorted and unprotected, into the wolf's territory surrounding the city walls. As legend goes, it wasn't long before the huge, shaggy beast came hurtling out of the woods directly toward Francis. But the young man faced it head-on. And over the ferocious animal, he

traced the sign of the Cross. The wolf reacted by falling meekly to its forepaws before Francis, who began to lecture the animal on the horrible consequences of its behavior. As Francis told it sternly, the act of laying violent paws on men and women, made in God's own sacred likeness, was worthy of capital punishment.

But Francis, always a peacemaker, struck a bargain with the wolf: if it agreed that it would never again harm the townsfolk or their livestock, he would ensure its survival. For its remaining days, it would be fed by the townspeople, and left alone and unharassed. To signal its agreement, the huge wolf placed its right paw in the hand of small Saint Francis.

As the story goes, Gubbio's citizens did in fact dutifully feed and care for the wolf, and the wolf was free to roam Gubbio's streets like a great tame dog. Such was the extent of the townsfolk's trust that the wolf was even allowed to enter their homes at will. And upon the wolf's death some years later, the residents of Gubbio mourned deeply. The animal that had been loved by Saint Francis received its own special burial.

[ABOVE] The Palazzo dei Consoli.
[OVERLEAF] *Gubbio: The Piazza,* oil on canvas, 93 x 42 inches.

Assisi: Basilica of Saint Francis, pen and ink.

ASSISI

CITY OF PEACE

I LACK SIMPLICITY. MY LIFE IS SO COMPLICATED, I SEEM TO BE FOREVER NEEDING SOMETHING. HELP ME TO SEE YOU LORD, AS DID CLARE AND FRANCIS, AS THE ALL-SUFFICIENT, AND THE END OF ALL OF MY LIFE. GIVE ME THE STRENGTH AND COURAGE TO SEEK YOU MORE THAN I SEEK MY OWN SELF. HELP ME TO LOVE THE POOR, TO SEE THE POOR, TO CARE FOR THE POOR BECAUSE YOU ARE THERE.

IF A SINGLE CITY IN ITALY COULD LAY CLAIM to being the most beloved destination of pilgrims from around the world, it would clearly be the medieval Umbrian town of Assisi.

Why can Assisi make such a claim? Because of the presence of Saint Francis of Assisi, which is still felt by residents and visitors to be not just a historical presence, but a living one. Although Saint Francis died and was buried in Assisi, a town he cherished deeply, in the early thirteenth century, visitors continue to bear witness to his loving, lingering spirit.

It is profoundly moving to witness how many people continue to stream to Assisi from every nation and religious tradition in the world, especially the teenagers and young adults. They come to pray at the tomb of the little poor man of Assisi, to revere him. They come in search of authentic spiritual inspiration from one who—in his own time—was much like themselves.

As a young man, Saint Francis reveled in a life of celebrations, social status, wealth, fame and glory. But he progressively came to see this existence as one preoccupied with passing, meaningless things. Ultimately, he chose to transform his reality by rejecting a life of materialism and triviality, and following his Master, Jesus Christ.

His renunciation of all that had formerly brought him happiness or status was heroic; his quest to serve his beloved Master without reserve was wholehearted. And in these actions Saint Francis became a model for all those who passionately seek the One who is the true Source of authentic love, peace, happiness and joy. The transparent single-heartedness of his love for God and for God's crea-

tures, all of whom he truly believed to be his sisters and brothers, continues to inspire.

When Pope John Paul II sponsored a World Day of Prayer for Peace in 1986, and invited leaders from the world's major religious traditions to participate, it was not to glorious Rome that he invited them, but to humble Assisi. Rome may still be linked in so many minds with imperial dominion or centralized ecclesiastical leadership, but Assisi is associated with a man universally recognized as a holy person of deep prayer, a peacemaker, a bridge-builder, a lover of God's creation.

The pilgrims and visitors who come to Assisi today in hopes of encountering Saint Francis find him everywhere. They see him in the beauty of the city's natural surroundings, the same surroundings that so delighted him. They discover him in their fellow men and women, be they citizens of the town or the pilgrims and visitors that come to Assisi seeking peace, God's forgiveness and reconciliation with others.

Traces of Saint Francis are also found in the historic places and monuments of Assisi, whether associated with his life or with the lives of his companions and followers.

The site of San Francesco Piccolo, once a stable, marks Saint Francis' birth in 1182. His mother, Donna Pica, had prophetically foreseen her child's future. She intentionally came to this lowly place so that Francis might be born—like Jesus—in poverty, among simple people and beasts.

The twelfth-century duomo or cathedral dedicated to Assisi's founding bishop, San Rufino, retains the baptismal font in which the child was baptized with the name Giovanni ("Francesco" was the nickname given later by his father). Thus he began his life as a disciple of Jesus Christ, and as a member of his Body, the Church.

[RIGHT] The hillside town of Assisi.

Alongside the town's original Cathedral of Santa Maria is located the Bishop's Palace, site of a pivotal, rather dramatic moment in Saint Francis's life. There, in sight of the bishop, his own father and a crowd of onlookers, he stripped himself of all his earthly possessions and entrusted himself completely to the providence of his Father in heaven. It was here that the young Francis formally began his religious quest.

At the rural church of San Damiano, Saint Francis received the famous message from the Icon of the Crucified Christ: "Go and repair my house, which is in ruins." Taking that command at its word, Francis went

begging stones from the townspeople. With these, he began to rebuild San Damiano's church, as well as another one dedicated to Saint Peter. He would later come to understand the symbolic meaning of Christ's charge to him: to restore and reinvigorate the Church of Christ.

The next church which Saint Francis rebuilt was the ancient chapel of Santa Maria degli Angeli, called the Porziuncola ("little portion"), which lay in the wooded valley below the city's walls, far removed from the town's center of power. After his work, Saint Francis received it in the form of a perpetual loan from the abbot of the Benedictine monks of Monte Subasio. This was his favorite dwelling place and, at his request, it would become the headquarters of the Franciscan Order. It was to the Porziuncola that he came to die, stretched naked on the bare earth, on October 3, 1226.

Francis' body was quickly taken within the walls of the city to protect it from the citizens of Perugia, who hoped to carry the saint's relics to their own town. He was buried in the church of San Giorgio, now incorporated into the monastery and basilica of Santa Chiara, headquarters of the feminine branch of the Franciscans. There, on July 16, 1228, he was canonized by Pope Gregory IX who the next day laid with his own hands the first stone of what would become the Basilica of Saint Francis.

On May 25, 1330, in that majestic basilica, St. Francis was finally laid to rest in the place he himself had chosen: a potter's field destined for the burial of executed criminals. His presence transformed the site: what was called the Colle inferiore ("lower hill"), or the Colle d'inferno ("hill of hell") is now rightly called the Colle del Paradiso ("hill of paradise").

[LEFT] The tomb of Saint Francis.
[OPPOSITE] *Assisi: The Basilica of Saint Francis,*
oil on canvas, 49 x 59 inches.

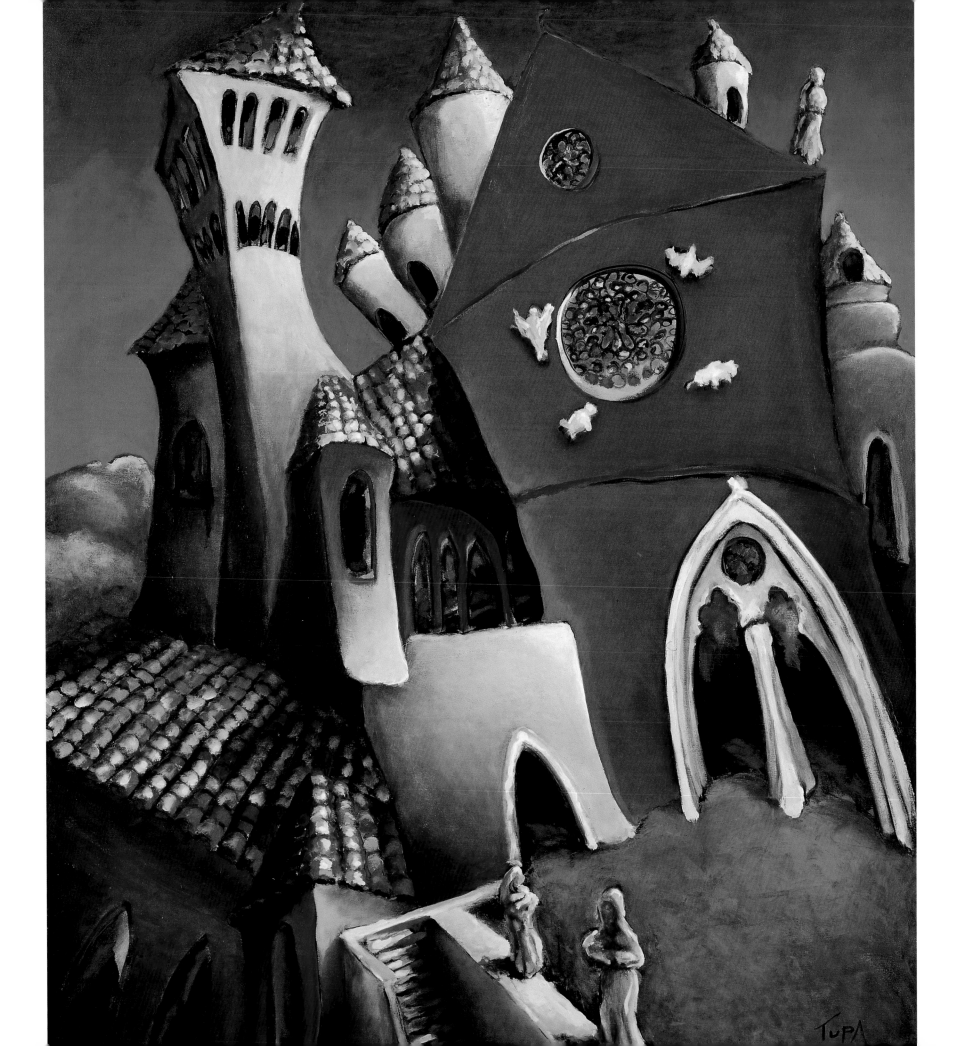

Most of the world-class art and architecture to be found in Florence is, in fact, religious in nature, or religiously inspired. In that sense, Florence presents a fascinating opportunity to explore the immense impact that faith and religion have had upon the arts. And with more than three million tourists coming to this smallish city (of some four hundred thousand) every year, there's a tremendous, constant exposure to some of the noblest religious themes and values found in Western culture. Explicitly or implicitly, those who spend time in Florence experience religion and faith as it's distilled in Florence's rich artistic heritage of the late Middle Ages and the Renaissance.

The arts and intellectual life already flourished in Florence by the 1300s. But with the Medici family's leadership from the early 1400s through the mid-1700s, the city would be transformed. The Medicis were utterly committed to supporting the arts and classical learning, as well as their own dynasty. The legendary Cosimo de' Medici became the ruler of Florence in 1434, and was then followed by a nephew who all but eclipsed the great Cosimo himself, Lorenzo "the Magnificent" whose rule (1469–1492) marked the period when Florence truly became the center of Italian humanism. Though the family went through major political ups and downs, most especially during the thirty-six-year span of

Santa Maria del Fiore prayer

Your duomo has a beautiful name, Our Lady of the Flower. Beautiful house, beautiful heritage should lead people to love what is beauty. All who pass like centuries of flowering spirits are touched by this place and our Lady. Bless you, whose face is all beauty. Bless you who created us in your own image!

FLORENCE

HEART OF THE RENAISSANCE

Florence as a Republic (1494–1530), Renaissance Florence is primarily Medici Florence.

The church known as the Medicis' own private church is that of San Lorenzo, built to house the family's mausoleum. There, adorning the tombs and altars of the Medicis, are some of Michelangelo's finest sculptures. Treated as an adopted son and vigorously sponsored by the family, Michalengelo's affection and gratitude are strongly displayed in these works. The public equivalent for the people of Florence is surely the great complex of its cathedral, baptistery and campanile (belltower). It is as much the civic center of the city as it is its religious heart. The very "Florentine" Gothic Duomo of Santa Maria del Fiore (constructed between the fourteenth and fifteenth centuries) was designed by Arnolfo di Cambio in 1296 and built over the site of the fourth-to-fifth-century Paleo-Christian church of Santa Reparata, the city's first Cathedral. When Brunelleschi completed his great dome in 1436, the cathedral of Florence became the first domed structure in Europe since Roman times. The great church was consecrated by Pope Eugene IV himself. For those attentive to oft-overlooked symbolic details, the cathedral's sanctuary area is octagonal in shape: This theologically inspired detail recalls the intimate connection between the Eucharist celebrated in the sanctuary at the altar, and baptism celebrated in the font of the octagonal baptistery.

The baptistery has an interesting story of its own. It was built in its present form in the eleventh century, in the traditional octagonal shape seen in many ancient baptisteries (such as that at Ravenna). Famous for its mosaics and figured bronze doors, it has been described as a Bible in pictures. Its south doors, dating from 1336, are the work of Andrea Pisano; its panels narrate the life of Saint John the Baptist. Its north doors, fashioned by Lorenzo Ghiberti and illustrating the life of Christ, took more than twenty-one

Florence's baptistery, cathedral and Giotto Tower.

years to complete. But Ghiberti's great east doors are the most renowned, with their remarkable gilded bronze panels. Ghiberti beat out seven others, including Brunelleschi and Michelangelo in a 1401 competition for their commission. Interestingly, Michelangelo was the one who later described Ghiberti's magnificent doors as the "Gate of Paradise." The doors' original panels are in the cathedral museum now, for their protection. They were nearly lost during a disastrous flood in 1966, but were found afterwards lodged behind some protective grillwork.

[ABOVE] One of the gilded bronze panels by Lorenzo Ghiberti from the east doors of the baptistry.

[OPPOSITE] *Florence: The Duomo*, oil on canvas, 64 x 76 inches.

Today's artistic pilgrims have endless opportunities to experience some of Florence's other shrines to art and architecture. There is the Galleria degli Uffizi, a magnificent building originally designed by Vasari as an administrative office for the Medicis. It houses what is perhaps the best collection of Renaissance paintings in the world. The Medici palaces of the Palazzo Vecchio and the Pitti, with its adjoining Boboli Gardens, are connected by a private covered passageway which runs over the Arno River by way of the Ponte Vecchio (1345). The Ponte Vecchio is the only bridge in Florence that survived destruction at the hands of the retreating German troops at the end of World War II, and is still known for its many goldsmith shops and crowds of tourists.

The Dominican monastery of San Marco is a veritable shrine to the two Dominican friars who once lived there. The artist Fra (Beato) Angelico decorated nearly every cell and common space in the monastery with his murals, and Fra Girolamo Savonarola, the fiery preacher, railed against the "vanities" that so enthralled the rest of Florence—as well as against the Medicis who sponsored them. He paid for his pro-Republic and anti-Renaissance zeal by being burned at the stake in the Piazza della Signoria in 1498.

No artistic pilgrimage would be complete without a trip to the Galleria dell' Accademia, which houses Michelengelo's *David* as well as the best collection of Michelangelo's works in the world. Unfortunately, today's pilgrim will have to view the *David* behind a thick sheet of bullet-proof glass, erected there to protect the statue, after it was damaged by a mentally disturbed tourist wielding a hammer.

Another one of Arnolfo di Cambio's projects, Florence's most prominent Franciscan church, Santa Croce (1295), is designed like the duomo in Florentine Gothic style. Ultimately, Brunelleschi completed the work in 1430. In many ways this is the Italian version of London's Westminster Abbey, housing the tombs and memorials of countless prominent Italians— Michelangelo, Galileo and Machiavelli among them. The exiled Dante was eventually granted a memorial in Santa Croce but is buried in Ravenna, where he died during his exile from Florence. One of the most fascinating and illuminating anecdotes connected with Santa Croce (and Florence itself) dates back to 1817, when the French novelist Stendahl, on artistic pilgrimage to Florence's many shrines, dramatically fainted outside the Niccolini Chapel. Apparently, he was overwhelmed by being exposed to too many masterpieces, too fast. (Of course, the Italians nodded approvingly.) His experience gave rise to the "Stendahl syndrome," as it is called in English, known in Italian as *Stendahlismo*: a marvelous description for what frequently overtakes visitors passing briefly through Florence. They are literally overwhelmed by the astonishing number of great buildings, beautiful scenery and world-class art concentrated in this one small town, the world's shrine to the Renaissance and humanism.

LUCCA

CITY OF THE HOLY FACE

I HAVE NEVER LIKED MY CROSS.

I HAVE ALWAYS FLED FROM SUFFERING.

I AM AFRAID TO SUFFER.

I CAN ONLY MAKE THE TRIP IF YOU GIVE ME STRENGTH.

YOU WHO HAVE CARRIED ALL OF OUR CROSSES.

I THANK YOU AND I BLESS YOU.

THE WALLED CITY OF LUCCA, now usually off the typical tourist path, was a well-known stop for centuries of pilgrims. In fact, for anyone on their way to Rome, whether for trade or sacred purposes—such as a pilgrimage to the Tombs of the Apostles—Lucca was a major crossroads, trade center and resting place. Lucca's ancient churches housed the relics of early Christian martyrs and saints. The city was particularly known for its miraculous and long-venerated image of Christ Crucified, the Volto Santo ("Holy Face" or "Holy Countenance").

Lucca's political history is an ancient one, dating back, like a number of other Italian cities, before Roman times. The area was settled in the Stone and Iron Ages before developing into an ancient Ligurian and then Etruscan population center. The name of the town itself derives from the Celtic-Ligurian word luk, which means "place of the marshes." Strategically, Lucca—unlike most other major Tuscan towns—was not built on an easily defended hill but on the unprotected, rather flat and marshy terrain near the Auser River. Such a location may have helped Lucca's early position as a trading center, but later it put the city at a disadvantage: Lucca continually found itself engaged in military skirmishes with its neighbors.

The town's close relationship with Rome began even before it formally became a Roman colony in 180 B.C.; it was quickly promoted to the rank of municipium, which gave it full status as a Roman city. From then on it would be intrinsically connected with the fortunes and misfortunes of the Roman Empire and then Republic: the first Roman Triumvirate of Caesar, Pompey, and Crassus had its seat in Lucca in 56 B.C.; by A.D. 476, when the Roman Empire fell, Lucca was conquered by Gothic tribes from the north. In 552 it was reconquered by troops of the Byzantine Emperor in an attempt to restore a united front to an Empire split between East and West. Significantly, it was under yet another of the northern tribes—the Longobards, who took over in 570, that Lucca began to flourish once more when it became the Duchy, or the seat of their king and the capital of Tuscia (Tuscany). Under the rule of the Longobards, Lucca experienced a genuine political, economic and cultural renaissance.

In the year 800 Charlemagne's Franks replaced the Longobards and created their own Marquisate of Tuscany.

[OPPOSITE] Lucca's duomo.
[OVERLEAF] *Lucca: Duomo*, oil on canvas, 93 x 42 inches.

THE ROAD TO ROME

Driving to Lucca from Florence was a piece of cake. Direct roads, a calm traffic flow and our little car keeping pace. We are headed for the cathedral, which has been a significant stop on the pilgrimage road for a millennium. After maneuvering through the city streets it was a challenge to find an available parking place. We prayed to Our Lady of the Parking Lot and ecco! Our own little space. I proceeded to find Il Duomo and set to work drawing the façade. Then it was on to the side view, and finally a drawing of the apse. After this work of about three hours I am thirsty and ready for a walk. But I stop inside the cathedral first. There, again, is that magnificent shrine to the Holy Cross. It is cool and dark here: I find myself just sitting and looking at this great structure and trying to feel the various moods and historical events that have taken place here. Perhaps most of the visitors are like myself. They stand in awe of this great human creation to the glory of God that has been respected and admired for eight hundred years. I am small. God is truly great. I hope I can create something worthy of this place.

Feudalism ruled until Lucca became an important free Commune, and the major rival of neighboring Pisa. Though by 1200 the Commune of Lucca was a major commercial player in Europe and beyond, in subsequent centuries Lucca's status faltered, rising and falling according to the outcome of continuous wars with Pisa, and ongoing battles between Guelphs and Ghibellines. The next centuries would see Lucca experience Pisan dominion, a single Lord over the Duchy, battles with Florence, revolts against the Emperor and the Medicis, a short-lived Republic ended by Napoleon's imposition of royalty, then Austrian rule, Bourbon rule and the unification of Italy as a single nation in 1870.

The Christian presence in Lucca was always closely related to the Church in Rome. Much like the founding of Christianity in Aquileia, the founding of the Church in Lucca is traced in local tradition to Saint Peter, bishop of Rome. In the case of Aquileia, the Evangelist Saint Mark is said to have selected a certain Ermacora from among his many converts to serve as the leader of Aquileia's new Christian community; Ermacora was brought to Rome, where Saint Peter appointed him the first bishop of Aquileia. In the case of Lucca, Christianity was brought to the town by San Paolino from Antioch, who had been converted to the faith by Saint Peter during Peter's time as that community's leader. Paolino, one of Peter's first disciples there, was later sent by Saint Peter to plant the Christian faith in Lucca for the sake of all Tuscany. Lucca, then, became a major regional missionary center for the promotion and diffusion of the faith.

Beyond the mythic accounts, the first documentary evidence of Christianity's establishment in Lucca is the presence of Bishop Maximus of Lucca at the Church Council of Sardica during A.D. 343–344. This information is extremely significant, as it points to evidence in those early years of Christianity as a religion tolerated by the Empire.

Not only do official records of the Council indicate Maximus' presence as the "Bishop of Lucca in Thuscia" (Tuscany), but other sources also list him as that city's eighth bishop, indicating a centuries-long Christian presence there already. And Lucca, like Rome, had its martyrs: Saint Regulus was specially venerated for his martyrdom at the hands of an Arian heretic. Regulus, an African bishop who came to live as a hermit in Tuscany, was decapitated on the orders of Gothic King Totila, himself an Arian Christian. The martyrdom underscores the fidelity of Lucca's Christianity to Roman orthodoxy, and points to longstanding religious conflicts in the area.

In its early days, when the city was still contained within its original Roman walls, there were four principal churches built outside the four main gates. Sadly, two of these ancient ecclesiastical jewels, the churches of San Pietro Maggiore and of San Donato, were destroyed during construction of Lucca's three-mile-long defensive walls (1544–1650). The two which remain are the church of Santa Maria Forisportam to the east, and the church of San Frediano to the west. The subject of so many pilgrimages to Lucca, the miraculous image of Christ Crucified, or Volto Santo, was once housed in the church of San Frediano.

In his "Leggenda Minor" the Deacon Leobino described the Volto Santo as "the most brilliant gem to decorate the crown of the Church of Lucca." Leobino dates the arrival of the Crucifix in Lucca to the eighth century, around the year A.D. 782, the time of Charlemagne's second year of ruling. The revered image of Christ was initially placed in the church of San Frediano outside the city walls. But over time it would be moved several times: first to its own separate shrine— sacello—dedicated to the Lord and Savior—*Domini et Salvatoris*— near the cathedral church of San Martino. By 930 the shrine had been destroyed and the relic was moved within the cathedral proper. In 1060, while the cathedral was being rebuilt, it was removed for ten years. Now, the pilgrim will find the sacred image in the cathedral again, housed in a small chapel or shrine that recalls its former one. On great feast days the life-sized polychromed carving of Christ is arrayed in a jeweled crown and precious vestments, which are otherwise on display in the cathedral's museum.

The cathedral church of San Martino is an ecclesiastical gem in itself, and houses a number of other gems as well. The church as it appears today is a uniquely Luccan version of the Romanesque style called Lucchese Romanesque. Built on the foundations of an earlier church, it was consecrated personally by Pope Alexander II (who was once Bishop Anselmo of Lucca) in 1170. Over the inside of the cathedral's main doors is a marvelous, life-sized thirteenth-century statuary group representing the cathedral's Patron, Saint Martin of Tours, as a Roman soldier on horseback, giving alms to a beggar.

The church of San Frediano is named for one of the many great saints venerated by pilgrims in Lucca for centuries. In the 590s, Pope Gregory the Great had already described him as a miracle worker. The church which now houses his relics was originally a primitive sixth-century church, built by San Frediano (or "Frigidian") himself to honor San Vincenzo, named the Basilica Longobardorum (Basilica of the Longobards) once that tribe took over Lucca. Bishop Giovanni later restructured the building and placed the relics of San Frediano there for the veneration of the faithful. In the twelfth century, Prior Rotone began the process of renovation; the church was consecrated by Pope Eugenius III in 1147. Later additions and renovations to the church date mainly from the fourteenth and sixteenth centuries. And for pilgrims visiting the church now, of particular interest is a relic of the Precious Blood of Jesus, which was at one time hidden in a hollow spot in the back of the Volto Santo.

TOWN OF TOWERS SAN

San Gimignano, watercolor, 30 x 22 3/8 inches.

GIMIGNANO

The term picturesque is so terribly overused throughout Italy. But in this walled gem of a town, that crowns the brow of its Tuscan hill, it truly fits. One can call this place *San Gimignano delle Belle Torri* (San Gimignano of the Beautiful Towers). And if it happens to evoke a hazy déjà vu, it's no accident. The Italian cinema genius Franco Zeffirelli may well be responsible. He filmed major segments of *Brother Sun, Sister Moon,* his acclaimed motion picture about the lives of Saints Francis and Clare of Assisi, here. The film's haunting opening scenes, though supposedly located in Assisi, were actually shot in San Gimignano, with its landmark towers rising from the fog-enshrouded hilltop.

More than its inherent beauty, San Gimignano's fame can be credited to its thirteen stone towers, which are all that's left of the seventy-two original towers that were built in the city's medieval glory days. Competing and warring noble families constructed them as symbols of their prominence.

The town of San Gimignano was prominent long before its famed towers rose toward the skies. Its legendary origins date back to Etruscan times (sixth century B.C.) when it was known as the town of Velathri, which was changed to Silvia in Roman times. Its current name is a corruption of San Geminiano (Saint Geminianus), the long-ago Bishop of Modena, who is credited with saving

[ABOVE] Piazza della Cisterna.
[RIGHT] *San Gimignano: The Towers*, oil on canvas, 59 x 49 inches.

SAN GIMIGNANO: 7/30/99

This is a city of towers, and some of the most beautiful and well-drawn frescoes I have ever seen. They recount the life of Jesus and the Last Judgement and are a feast for the eyes. As I sit sketching in the hot sun at the edge of the square, a very old woman with a great smile approaches and says, "How lovely!" I smile in return and thank her for the kind words. The church bells begin to ring and she suggests I attend the Mass. I accept this as another angel, and leave my work to join her. As I take her arm to help her up the steps, Maria tells me she is ninety years old, but still strong enough to climb the fifteen steps without stopping. Her gaze is full of wisdom and her wrinkled skin seems to glow. Once inside, she disappears towards the front as the service begins. I, the typical Catholic, sit in the rear. I am moved by Maria's devotion and seeming calm.

San Gimignano: Summer Heat, oil on canvas, 76 x 64 inches.

the town from Gothic attacks. Devotion to the saintly Bishop of Modena, centered in the sixth-century church housing his relics, eventually contributed to the decision to change the town's name in his honor.

Thankfully for its inhabitants, San Gimignano was strategically located on the Via Francigena, the main pilgrimage route from northern Europe to the Tombs of the Apostles Peter and Paul in Rome. So the formerly quiet little farming town, which had depended almost solely on agricultural production, quickly became a bustling center of commerce and religion with a thriving merchant class. Its populace profited not only from a steady stream of devout pilgrims, but from the worldly travelers and merchants who passed through as well, seeking shelter and meals and patronizing the town's shops.

In an age characterized by spiritual devotion, and the genuine horror of the great plagues, which cost the town up to half its population, there was great interest in religious monuments. Those containing the relics of major saints or notable works of art were given special importance, and San Gimignano's Pieve or Collegiata church gathered within its walls many sacred attractions.

The current church was started in the eleventh century and modified in the fourteenth. It's likely that it occupies the original site of the sixth-century church that was dedicated to the bishop San Geminiano. Of special note are the frescoes covering the walls of its nave, particularly the *Last Judgment* scene executed in 1393 by Taddeo di Bartolo. Its principal architectural and devotional gem is the fifteenth-century Chapel of Santa Fina, named for one of the city's most saintly citizens. Fina de' Ciardi died at the age of fifteen on March 12, 1253. She had led a life remarkable for its holy penitence and is, arguably, the city's proudest boast.

Historically speaking, it was in the Collegiata that the fiery reformer Fra Girolamo Savonarola preached during

The Salvucci Towers.

the Lenten seasons of 1484 and 1485, long before he had attained renown and the adherence of his fellow Florentine citizens. And San Bartolo, another of the city's most holy citizens, is venerated here. Bartolo dedicated his life to caring for medieval Europe's most feared and hated group: its lepers. (He's buried in the thirteenth-century church of Sant' Agostino, in a chapel erected in his honor by the town's leading citizens.)

Beyond its religious context, San Gimignano is full of impressive architectural and historic monuments, such as the thirteenth-century Palazzo Comunale located to the left of the Collegiata. The Palazzo's 174-foot-tall civic bell tower is the tallest in the city, and marks the site where, in 1300, Dante was received as an ambassador when he came to persuade the city (unsuccessfully) to join the Tuscan League. Directly across the piazza from the Collegiata is the fourteenth-century Palazzo della Podestà, the residence of the town's governors. Its 167-foot-tall tower indicated the maximum height to which individual families' towers could be built. In Zeffirelli's film, the Palazzo was the home of Saint Francis of Assisi's family.

HOME OF SAINT CATHERINE
SIENA

Siena, watercolor, 24 1/4 x 18 inches

Catherine heard voices calling for peace and change. By her faith, she is an example of a courageous woman dedicated to peace, justice and the constant reform of the Church. Help us who pass this way, and hear the bell named Maria Assunta to be enlivened and encouraged, no matter how weak or how insignificant we seem. For God is a friend to all who call.

Siena's zebra-striped duomo.

Siena! A city renowned for its world-class art and architecture; for its *Palio*, the famed annual horse race held since the early 1300s in the unique fan-shaped Campo piazza; for its *panforte*, a medieval fruitcake still enjoyed by Sienese and tourists alike; and for much more. But ask any Christian pilgrim what gives Siena its greatest cause for renown and the reply will always be the same: Saint Catherine. For Siena is, above all, the city of Caterina Benincasa, Saint Catherine of Siena, who along with Francis of Assisi is the co-patron saint of Italy.

Caterina Benincasa was born in 1347, the youngest child of Giacomo Benincasa and his wife, Monna Lapa. In a family already "rich with children," Catherine quickly set herself apart by demonstrating a spiritual maturity far beyond her natural years. So impressive was her spirituality that, when she decided to forsake marriage, it overcame her parents' opposition. Thus she was able to consecrate herself wholly to the spouse she always called her *Cristo dolce Gesù* (Christ sweet Jesus).

Catherine donned the veil and habit of a lay Dominican and began to live a secluded life within the walls of her family home. In the first years of her conversion, she rarely left the house, except on her customary visits to the nearby Basilica of San Domenico, where she spent lengthy periods in prayer and contemplation. There she celebrated her heavenly nuptials with Christ and mystically exchanged hearts with him. If Catherine of Siena is known at all to contemporary Christians, it is most likely for those mystical experiences and doctrines which contributed to her being named the first female Doctor of the Church.

Catherine's living relationship with her divine Spouse overflowed into an equally deep love for Christ's Body—the Church—and especially for its neediest members. She was as well known in her day for her tender love and care of the sick and the poor as she was for her mystical marriage and sanctity. Her loving concern

This city certainly has its multicolored charm. As I was sitting in the Campo painting, I became aware of a quiet presence beside me. He occasionally looked at my watercolor as he worked on a drawing himself.

"Do you draw here often?" he finally asked me.

"No," I replied, "this is my first time."

"Me too!" he exclaimed.

Davide is his name; he is about eight years old and a real hard worker when it comes to drawing. His mom and dad took care of his two-year-old sibling while they watched with love as their son drew just like the old man he had found as a companion.

Davide is on vacation and was looking forward to serving mass that Saturday evening. What a blessed child! When his parents told me they were part of a lay religious group that cares for youth in various cities in Italy, I felt warm and embraced by their broad smiles and warm eyes. If they are representative of this dedicated group, then they will certainly bring peace and joy to their communities. I felt as though Davide was in my path for a reason.

That evening at about eight o'clock my friends and I were sitting in a little pizzeria near our hotel when out of the blue I hear a bright voice calling "Ciao Girolamo!" And there was Davide passing with his parents. He came over to shake my hand with an assurance and comfort that belied his eight years.

"Are you painting tomorrow?" he asked.

"No, we are off to another pilgrimage site," I replied.

He seemed sad, and simply said, "Ciao! Ciao!"

I should love to have a child like this.

An angel has crossed my path.

quickly grew into a desire for peace and reconciliation, initially among the warring families and factions of her beloved Siena, and then throughout troubled Italy and Christendom itself.

Intervening as a mediator between warring cities and regions close to home, she eventually counseled more dis-
tant leaders and communities to work for peace. In an era which permitted women little or no political participation, Catherine was universally respected as one who, for the love of Christ and Christ's Church, did not hesitate to lecture popes and worldly rulers on the need to reform the horrendous abuses of both Church and society.

Siena: Campo, watercolor, 30 x 22 inches.

Many of Saint Catherine's relics are found in Rome, where she died in 1380. Located in the church of Santa Maria Sopra Minerva, near the Pantheon, they are contained in a life-sized polychromatic image of the saint, which lies under the glass-sided high altar. But pilgrims and visitors to Siena will nevertheless find a city marked in many ways by Catherine's presence. Her family home was long ago transformed into a sanctuary and her most famous relics are deposited in the nearby thirteenth-century Basilica of San Domenico, looking much the same as Catherine herself would have seen it. These include the sacred relic of her head, contained in a marble tabernacle

Siena's Piazza del Campo.

Siena: San Domenico, watercolor, 24¹/₄ x 18 inches.

sculpted by Giovanni di Stefano in 1466, and the relic of her finger, which the peacemaker so often used to wag at popes and other rulers.

While Siena's duomo is not a major site of pilgrimage in terms of Saint Catherine, it is still one of the most impressive religious constructions in Italy. Commissioned in 1136, the cathedral was only "finished" in 1314. In the first half of the fourteenth century, following one of Siena's most prosperous periods, the Sienese intended to enlarge the cathedral and began construction of the Duomo Nuovo. But the 1348 plague which devastated the city quickly brought work to a permanent halt.

The duomo contains works of art by Jacopo della Quercia, Lorenzo Ghiberti (famous for his "Doors of Paradise" on Florence's Baptistery), Nicola Pisano, Vecchietta, Peruzzi, Donatello, Michaelangelo, Matteo di Giovanni, Pinturicchio and Bernini, to name a few.

The most notable decorative elements of the cathedral are its black-and-white marble columns and walls; the 172 sculpted Papal portraits supporting the cornice; the busts of 36 Emperors; a unique, Renaissance polychromatic marble mosaic pavement; the Piccolomini Library, with its third-century Roman statue of the *Three Graces* and the important fresco cycle (1505–1508) by Pinturicchio (Bernardino di Betto, 1454–1513); the chapel (1661); the miraculous image of the Madonna del Voto

Siena: San Domenico, oil on canvas, 59 x 49 inches.

(Sienese from the 1200s); and the baptistery (Pieve di San Giovanni) with its font, a masterpiece of fifteenth-century sculpture.

Although not strictly a destination for pilgrims, the city's fan-shaped central piazza (the *campo*, site of the yearly *Palio* horse race) was where the revered San Bernardino da Siena used to preach to huge crowds from the balconies of the public buildings. The fiery Franciscan friar was the most famous preacher and reformer of his time, which straddled the fourteenth and fifteenth centuries. Among

Siena's devout citizens, he was second only in veneration to Saint Catherine herself.

Looming over the *campo* is the city's most visible landmark, the great Torre del Mangia bell tower (built between 1338 and 1348). Its huge bell, the Campanone (big bell) or Sunto (short for Assunta after the Assumption of the Blessed Virgin Mary) was forged and baptized in 1665, and named Maria Assunta.

CORTONA

VINTNER'S DELIGHT

Lovely little town set on a hill,
surrounded by ramparts and towers.
You catch the noonday sun.
Do you feel us walking on your streets?
Am I heavy?
Is my painting right?
Did I catch you at the right moment?

Elsewhere in this book, in the chapter on the town of Urbania, there's a quote from the local archbishop. Referring to Urbania's local patron saint, whose relics are housed in the cathedral, he said, "To speak of Urbania is also to speak of Saint Christopher." It is much the same way in Cortona. Rising some seven hundred meters above the plains of the Val di Chiana, this ancient town is inextricably connected to Santa Margherita. Particularly for

[ABOVE] *Cortona*, watercolor, 24¼ x 18 inches.
[OPPOSITE] Cortona's La Loggetta.

pilgrims, to speak of Cortona is to speak of Santa Margherita da Cortona.

Cortona originally saw the presence of the Umbrans, Etruscans and Romans, later witnessed the establishment of the Christian Church in the late third century, along with the martyrdom of its founding bishop, Vincenzo, and grew in the faith and presence of Saint Francis of Assisi himself. But when the pilgrims climb to Cortona, it is indisputably Santa Margherita whom they seek.

Santa Margherita's bodily remains lie enshrined in the church dedicated to her sacred memory. The residents of Cortona regard her as their great patron and protector. But even beyond the confines of this Tuscan hill town, famed for its artistic native sons—Lucca Signorelli and Pierta da Cortona—the memory of Santa Margherita is held in the highest esteem by millions of the Catholic faithful, who refer to her as the "Third Sun" of the Franciscan Order. She is third only after the Order's first and second suns, Saints Francis and Clare of Assisi. And the story of Margherita's road to sanctity is one of the most unusual, and moving, of Italy's many saints.

Margherita was born in 1247, not in the Cortona that

has come to be identified with her, but far down the hills, in the Val di Chiana at Laviano, near Lake Trasimeno. Her parents viewed her birth as a gift from God, and loved her in a way that few female children were loved at that time. But when Margherita was only eight years old her seemingly ideal family life was disrupted by the unexpected death of her mother. Her father remarried a woman who initially had little time for Margherita. Soon, giving birth to a child of her own, the stepmother had no time for her husband's first daughter at all, and Margherita's existence in her own home became unbearable.

It was no surprise to anyone, then, that at the age of sixteen she secretly left home to live with a young nobleman named Arsenio from Montepulciano. He was the first man who had paid her any real attention and he was deeply in love with her.

Sadly, the young girl's dreams of the perfect romance and marriage would never come to fruition. Arsenio expected all the benefits of a wedded relationship without wanting to enter into the formal, sacramental bonds of marriage. They had a child together, but Margherita's pleas for a lawful marriage were continually put off by Arsenio with one excuse after another. Nine years after they'd come to live together, Arsenio's body was found in the fields where he had gone on a hunting expedition. His death was a mystery. His family immediately evicted the unwanted Margherita and her child from their home, leaving the twenty-five-year-old unwed mother to fend for herself. She was forced to return to Laviano, to beg hospitality from her paternal home. Apparently at the insistence of her stepmother, she was refused. She and her child were alone: no resources, and nowhere to go.

Bereft, the young woman stood gazing at the town of Cortona, which sat high on a hill in the distance. She perceived an inner voice which assured her that she should go to that hill; there, she would be told what to do. So she

went to Cortona and was given refuge in the family home of two maiden sisters of the Moscari family.

Initially Margherita worked in the Moscari sisters's household as a servant to repay their generosity. But within a short time, the simple rooms assigned to her use were being visited continually by the poor and the sick of the village. Margherita received them with immense love and ministered to them with legendary compassion. The care and healing they received at her hands went far beyond their corporal needs, and Margherita's reputation as a miracle worker grew.

Margherita still suffered from pangs of guilt for the nine years she'd lived out of wedlock with her lover. Seeking spiritual guidance and relief, she began to make regular visits to the church of San Francesco, where she chose Father Giunta Bevegnati as her confessor. The choice was providential: Giunta, a holy old friar who would later become Margherita's biographer, assisted her with tender mercy and understanding as she struggled with her own sense of her unworthiness to receive God's forgiveness. With Father Giunta's spiritual direction Margherita came to experience the forgiveness she longed for, and with it an intense desire to give herself completely to the service of God. She would do so by serving the poorest and neediest. As a direct result of Margherita's fervor and apostolic zeal, a number of Cortona's wealthiest families cooperated in her ministry, and helped her to found the Hospital of Santa Maria della Misericordia. The hospital still exists, now renowned and much expanded, carrying on the ministry started more than seven hundred years ago by Margherita herself.

As the years passed, Margherita experienced an ever-deepening, more urgent desire to be one with God. She was received as a member of the Third Order of Saint Francis of Assisi and later moved into a small cell at the rear of the church of San Basilio. There, she spent her final years in mystical contemplation. It is said that she engaged in regular, personal dialogues with God. Through personal repentance and compassion for the poorest of God's poor, the public sinner had attained a mystical state of union with God experienced by few saints in the history of Christianity. That loving union, overflowing into the lives of those she served, became a source of the countless healings and miracles that made Margherita the trusted spiritual friend of the people of Cortona.

Margherita's shrine continues to draw the faithful, both from Cortona and beyond, who come to pray at her tomb in what is now the church of Santa Margherita, alongside the former church of San Basilio where she spent her last years in seclusion. She died on February 22, 1297. Immediately, the people of Cortona acclaimed her as a saint.

The significance of Margherita's story can hardly be lost on the pilgrims and faithful of our own time; indeed, it seems especially relevant now. For contemporary men and women to know that there is a saint in Cortona who has shared so many of their own difficult experiences, and prevailed with extraordinary spiritual success, is encouraging beyond telling. In particular, Margherita's experience of being a single mother—rejected by her own family and left to care for herself and for her child—seems to offer people in similar circumstances a patron who understands the difficulties and pains of such a predicament. Perhaps, even more importantly, her story provides people with a patron who may have been discounted by her society but who, nonetheless, triumphed in her desire to grow in personal sanctity. She never forgot to care for her fellow women and men in equally distressing situations. In her extraordinary life shines out the message of God's infinite mercy and forgiveness.

CORTONA: 8/6/99

Cortona sits on a hill overlooking the vineyards that make this area so famous. It is the region of Brunello wine. When we arrived, we had to park in the garage that belongs to our hotel, on the smallest, narrowest street imaginable. Trying to make the turn into this garage was next to impossible. There were two other cars already at the trough snorting their oats. My car somehow decided it didn't like this place, and hit the wall. (Why do cars do those things?)

That afternoon, sitting up on the top steps of the city hall, I had a great view of an Italian evening scene. The passeggiata. All of the youth of the town seem to stream through in little bands, holding hands or shoulders, stopping to greet each other in their groups. Children run noisily about. Husbands and wives stroll. Men sit at a bar and ogle. Young women giggle. It seems like a well-rehearsed drama, friendly and warm. I am secure in my drawing, though I notice that people look at me as if I were somehow to be pitied. I am alone, it's true, a state which is really the bane of the Italian psyche. Being alone is unheard of. Yet I am entirely content.

[OVERLEAF] *Cortona: La Loggetta*, oil on canvas, 93 x 42 inches.

LA LOGGETTA

WHERE ART MEETS FAITH

ORVIETO

H OW CAN I PRAISE YOU AS THESE GREAT SAINTS DID?
HOW CAN I MEASURE UP TO THEIR HIGH STANDARDS?
HOW CAN I BE A REAL PERSON OF DEEP FAITH AND PRAYER?
I CANNOT LIVE ON A MOUNTAIN TO PROVE MY LOVE.
I CANNOT LIVE IN A CAVE TO FIND QUIET.
HELP ME TO FIND PEACE, JOY AND QUIET IN YOUR HEART
THAT IS A MOUNTAIN OF LOVE IN MY WORLD.

The abbey in the hills near Orvieto.

IN ALL OF ITALY there are few cities as exotic-looking as Orvieto, or so remarkable for the utter majesty of their location. The town rises from the level crest of its sheer vertical-sided plateau like some medieval Disneyland, miraculously transported to Umbria and reminiscent, somewhat, of the expansive mesas in the great American Southwest.

Orvieto's strategic significance—its virtually inaccessible elevation and therefore easily defended site—was apparent even to this region's earliest inhabitants. The town was settled by a steady stream of peoples, successively occupied by Etruscans, Romans, Goths, Byzantines and Lombards before it became one of those proudly independent medieval communes or city-states in the eleventh and twelfth centuries. It long remained a known Guelph stronghold, repeatedly serving as a papal refuge from the political upheavals that frequently plagued the

city of Rome. Over time, more than thirty-three popes reportedly took residence there.

Tourists flock to Orvieto to marvel at its amazing location and design—the massive city walls that encircle and protect the town, the fortresses, monasteries, churches and public buildings. But Orvieto's chief monument is its duomo, or cathedral, an unparalleled architectural and artistic gem. Here one may grasp, perhaps better than anywhere else, the intricate interrelationship between art and faith.

Christian pilgrims regard the duomo with particular reverence, as it is the repository of one of Christendom's most sacred relics. In fact, the great church was actually built specifically as a shrine to house the relic of the "Holy

124

[ABOVE] *Orvieto: East*, watercolor, 29³/₄ x 22³/₁₆ inches.
[OVERLEAF] *Orvieto*, oil on canvas, 93 x 42 inches.

Corporal." A corporal is the small linen altar cloth upon which the Body (*corpus* in Latin) and Blood of Christ rest during the Mass. Orvieto's famous corporal is deemed holy because, during the "Miracle of Bolsena," it was stained with the very Blood of Christ. Bolsena, site of the miracle, is a small town located near Orvieto along the famous Via Francigena pilgrimage route to Rome. For centuries it has been a prominent destination of pilgrims in its own right, because of its church of Santa Cristina, which houses the revered relics of the young, martyred saint of the early Church. It was in Santa Cristina's church that the Miracle of Bolsena occurred.

In A.D. 1263, Peter of Prague, a priest, was returning home from his pilgrimage to the Tombs of the Apostles Peter and Paul in Rome. He stopped in Bolsena to venerate the relics of Santa Cristina. Contemporary accounts describe him as a good priest, but one who struggled with doubts regarding the Real Presence of Christ in the Sacrament of the Eucharist. It was during his celebration of Mass at the saint's tomb that the miracle happened: As the Host was broken in preparation for its distribution at Holy Communion, it began to bleed into the priest's hands. So profuse was the flow of blood that it soaked the square of fair linen upon which the chalice and Host rested. Needless to say, the priest's doubts were dispelled and word spread quickly of the astonishing event.

Pope Urban IV, then in residence at the papal palace in Orvieto, requested the bloodstained corporal be brought to him for careful examination. He was moved so deeply by what he saw that he ordered Thomas of Aquinas, in Orvieto as a professor of theology for his fellow Dominican friars, to compose hymns and praises in honor of the Eucharist. Thus the Eucharistic hymns still sung by the Church in adoration of Christ, present in the Sacrament of the Altar, are a direct result of this thirteenth-century miracle.

Pope Urban also commanded that a sanctuary be built to house the miraculous Eucharistic relic. The ensuing Duomo of Orvieto is credited to the day's finest architects, builders, craftsmen and artists. In *The Story of Perugia*, the great cathedral is described by authors Symonds and Gordon as "a peacock in a hen-coop, a miracle of marbles and mosaics... a dream in stone." And Pope John XXIII is quoted as saying, "On the day of judgement the angels will descend on Orvieto to transport the Duomo to heaven—lest it be destroyed."

ORVIETO: 8/10/99

As a pilgrim walking up the steep grade towards the cathedral there are about seven or eight chapels on the way that help me recollect my thoughts and place me in the Presence.

It is difficult to know what thread draws us along through life. Certainly, the search for love is at the very heart of each person's journey, creating great moments of joy and even bliss. Yet at other times there is sorrow and almost despair at being so alone. A pilgrimage brings us along all of these paths in one series of events that finally arrives at a singular goal such as a city or a shrine. Walking up the hillside to arrive at the great cathedral of Orvieto fills me with fatigue under the heavy sun. Cars rush past and startle me, but occasionally I catch a glimpse of the church and my hope revives.

Why this journey to Rome? That must be a daily question. Upon finally arriving at the church in Orvieto, somehow the object of this trip becomes clear once again. On the road we must move from desire to compassion, from our centered thoughts to a universal vision, so that we can speak out and embrace all of creation.

Orvieto: Duomo and Post Office, pen and ink.

Orvieto: City Walls, watercolor, 29 7/8 x 22 3/16 inches.

The duomo's extraordinary collection of art is one of its most important contributions to popular theology. Surrounding the lower rank of the cathedral's towering, mosaic-covered façade are four polygonal piers covered with matchless, fourteenth-century marble bas-reliefs usually attributed to the sculptor Maitani. The impressively detailed panels depict the Creation, Messianic Prophecies and various New Testament scenes. But the portion that depicts the Last Judgment in horrendous detail is considered the most significant by art historians. Famous even in their own day, these reliefs influenced many subsequent artistic and theological interpretations of the story, most notably Michelangelo's masterpiece in the Sistine Chapel, and Luca Signorelli's frescoes in the Capella Nuova of the duomo itself.

Inside the church's great nave, pilgrims and visitors make their way to the most notable attractions housed within its black-and-white striped marble walls: the chapels of the Holy Corporal and San Brizio, known as the Capella Nuova. The sacred goal of the pilgrims who visit the sanctuary is the Holy Corporal, encased within a silver-gilded, enameled and jeweled reliquary shrine. With its doors kept open, the corporal can be freely viewed and venerated by the faithful. After more than seven hundred years, the dark, rust-colored stains of Christ's Precious Blood are still visible on the yellowed linen. The shrine is a masterpiece of medieval art, housed in a beautiful carved marble frame that rises above the chapel's altar. As beautiful as the chapel's historic frescoes may be, the sacred corporal is what receives the hushed attention of the pilgrims, who gather before it in prayerful adoration and wonder.

Those who enter Orvieto's duomo on an "artistic pilgrimage" tend to seek out the breathtaking frescoes found in its chapel of San Brizio. These works were actually begun by Fra Angelico, but the artist was so overwhelmed

The facade of Orvieto's duomo.

by other commissions that he resigned his commission for Orvieto, and withdrew with the work barely started. Luca Signorelli was commissioned to complete the work, which may have been providential—his amazing approach probably never would have occurred to the more conventional Dominican friar.

Signorelli expressed his own interpretations of the ancient biblical themes of the coming of Antichrist and the Last Judgment in shocking detail and gloriously vivid colors. There is Antichrist, suavely persuading naïve Christians that evil is, in fact, good, and mercilessly leading those who see through him and resist him to their martyrs' deaths. There are the dead, who at the blast of the angel's trumpet blast literally crawl out of their earthen graves in every possible state of decomposition. There are the blessed, resurrected to be carried aloft in loving angels' arms to heaven, where they sing God's praises in the company of angels and saints. There are the damned, resurrected to be hauled down to hell by hideous, bat-winged demons, that revel in tormenting their new comrades bereft of all hope. All of it is displayed before the astonished gaze of the chapel's dumbstruck visitors.

[ABOVE] *Subiaco: Santa Scolastica*,
watercolor, 22¼ x 30 inches.

[OPPOSITE] *Subiaco: Santa Scolastica*, oil on canvas, 49 x 59 inches.

Holy ground of mountains and caves. Help us to hear the silence of your breathing in the nature around us. St. Benedict walked here, St. Scholastica walked here. Saints are supposed to walk, and stop, and pray here. Where are they? Why do I only see my footsteps, sunk in the dirt?

THE DRAMATIC DESTRUCTION of the ancient Benedictine Abbey of Monte Cassino by Allied bombing raids at the end of World War II ironically assured the worldwide fame of that "cradle of the Benedictine Order." Reports of the monastery's leveling were plastered across the headlines of newspapers and newsreel screens around the globe. Even those who were little familiar with Benedictine monks and nuns, or with the Benedictine Order's rich, fifteen-century history, closely followed the story with interest and dismay.

In stark contrast, the Benedictine Abbey of Subiaco never achieved such notoriety, and continues in its state of relative anonymity just outside of Rome. But if Monte Cassino is the "cradle of the Benedictine Order" then Subiaco was its "spiritual womb." Here is where the young Saint Benedict actually began his life as a monk, before he went to Monte Cassino where he continued his remarkable monastic career.

SUBIACO
A SPIRITUAL WOMB

Benedict and his twin sister, Scholastica, were born into a middle-class family near the Umbrian town of Nursia (now known as Norcia) around A.D. 480. Very little is known of the twins' childhood and early adolescence. But in accordance with the standard Roman custom of the time, the family sent the boy to Rome for the standard course of classical studies, while his sister was given into the care of a community of consecrated women. Scholastica fades for a time from history, until she reappears as a holy woman herself. Benedict's later life was chronicled by his biographer, Pope Saint Gregory the Great.

According to Gregory, Benedict's academic career in Rome was short-lived. Wise beyond his years, and already committed to the service of God, the young Benedict quickly grew disenchanted with Rome's moral and civic deterioration. Withdrawing from his course of studies, he abandoned the Capital, seeking a tranquil place in which he could spend time in prayerful reflection on his next step. He found just such a place in a little village located in the hills surrounding Rome.

But Benedict's sojourn in that town was almost as brief as his Roman stay. Upset by the unwanted admiration of local villagers, who called attention to his reputation as a worker of holy wonders, he ventured farther into the wilderness. Eventually he came to the site of Emperor Nero's abandoned country villa of Sub Lacum ("below the lake")—today's Subiaco. That was around A.D. 500, more than fifteen hundred years ago.

The would-be recluse was quite unprepared for the wild conditions he encountered at Subiaco, and providentially was discovered by a local monk named Romanus. Young as he was, Benedict's religious sincerity so impressed the veteran monk that he immediately invested the young man with the traditional monastic garb of a basic tunic and leather belt. With that simple, ancient ritual, Benedict formally began his monastic vocation. Romanus subsequently led him to a cave hidden high on the sheer rock wall of a cliff overlooking the green gorge of the river Aniene and Nero's villa, far below. In that secluded spot, Benedict dwelt alone and in secret, fed on the meager food that Romanus spirited away from his monastery and lowered to the hide-out on the end of a rope. For three years Romanus alone knew of the existence of the young hermit whose life was spent in prayer, ascetic practice, and deepening his awareness of the presence of God.

Saint Gregory writes that Benedict's first human encounter, beyond Romanus' regular food drops, occurred when God revealed the hermit's presence to a local priest. It was Easter Sunday and the priest was preparing to break his Lenten fast with a festal meal. God told the cleric that he could hardly dine without guilt while Benedict was in desperate need of nourishment, both culinary and human, and commanded the priest to seek Benedict immediately. The startled priest did seek out the man of God. And then, with difficulty, he convinced Benedict that it really was Easter, and that he could indeed relax his severe fast to celebrate the great Feast.

Following that divinely ordered Easter visit, a group of local shepherds stumbled upon Benedict's cave by sheer chance and were nearly frightened to death, mistaking the unshaven, fur-clothed monk for a wild beast. Benedict first calmed them, then reluctantly agreed to the shepherds' plea for instruction in the Christian faith. He permitted them to return for that instruction on a regular basis, but now his hidden dwelling place and his secret existence were well known. He would never again enjoy the fruitful solitude of those three years spent in his beloved cavern, which for centuries afterwards pilgrims called the *Sacro Speco* (sacred cavern).

Before he left Subiaco and moved, ultimately, to Monte Cassino near Naples, Benedict founded a dozen

Subiaco: Sacro Speco, watercolor, 30 x 22⁷/₁₆ inches.

Subiaco: Sacro Speco, watercolor, 35⁹/₁₆ x 24 inches.

Subiaco: Santa Scolastica, pen and ink.

monasteries at Subiaco, each with a dozen monks and an abbot that he personally appointed. One by one, over the course of the centuries, the small monasteries were abandoned. Today there remains only one large monastery known as the Abbey of Santa Scolastica, and the smaller monastic community that houses the monks who care for the sacred cave, on the hill above the abbey.

Historically, the Abbey of Monte Cassino would become increasingly important and claim more attention from pilgrims than Subiaco. A major factor was that both Benedict and Scholastica are buried there, and thus the abbey became a major shrine and pilgrimage site. But Monte Cassino also had a growing impact on Western Christianity, producing numerous saints, scholars and popes, and exerting tremendous influence in the area of spirituality, liturgy and academics. Monte Cassino's contribution to the development of medieval Christianity and western civilization in general can hardly be exaggerated.

But what of Subiaco? In no way was it eclipsed. Rather, it became an extremely significant place in its own right, a proving ground for major innovations in medieval and Renaissance art, architecture and technology. The Abbey of Subiaco commissioned some of the first, and finest, examples of Romanesque architecture, such as its famous campanile, the "Cosmatesque" inlaid marble of its cortile and chiostro, and Gothic structures such as the monumental gateway leading into the abbey's second-oldest cortile. The monastery's magnificent buildings were themselves further enriched by some of Christendom's finest painters and sculptors.

And it was the Abbey of Subiaco that housed the first printing press after Gutenberg's, set up at Santa Scolastica by two German printers. At Subiaco these printers produced Italy's first printed texts before eventually moving their operation to Rome. Original copies of those texts are

SUBIACO: 8/15/99

Blessed is the pilgrim privileged to spend time at prayer in this sacred place. Blessed is the pilgrim able to leave behind the noise of the city and make the journey to Subiaco's green mountains. Subiaco is a place whose silence is broken only by the sounds of the river, rushing over the time-worn rocks in the valley far below. It's a place whose silence is broken only by the song of birds startled awake by the rising sun of a new day, and the chant of Benedict's monks, who still punctuate the hours of each day with their canticles of divine praise.

still in the abbey's library, part of a collection of rare manuscripts and irreplaceable printed books that is a researcher's dream.

Far more than a mere treasure house for art and architecture, Subiaco remains a pilgrim's destination. While deeply impressed by the history and beauty of the Abbey of Santa Scolastica, pilgrims are inevitably drawn farther up the rugged mountain to Benedict's sacred cavern, which is often poetically described as a kind of "swallow's nest." It is surrounded by buildings constructed by the monks over the course of fifteen hundred years, which form a unique jewel of medieval and Renaissance art and architecture. And at the very heart of that jewel, stark and unadorned in the midst of so much decoration, is the living rock of the cave. It is an awesome place: palpably sacred and immensely significant.

ROME
THE ETERNAL CITY

Here on this spot where an angel appeared,
I am in awe of our good fortune,
To know that God is with us.
Our journey is not solitary.
It is filled with people who are messengers of God's love,
Messengers who strengthen us,
Messengers who keep us on the path.
Thank you for the gift of angels.
May we never disappoint them,
Or weary them.

AD LIMINA APOSTOLORUM! "To the thresholds of the Apostles!" This has been the pious cry and goal of a seemingly endless stream of pilgrims who have made their way to Rome from every corner of the known world. They have journeyed to this city since the earliest days of Christianity and they journey there still, by the millions.

But why Rome, of all places? Rome, that was the "head" of the pagan Roman Empire, whose Emperor claimed to be a god himself. Rome, that was responsible for the crucifixion of Jesus. Rome, that barely thirty years after Jesus' death, besieged and destroyed the Holy City of Jerusalem itself. Rome, whose ravaging army dispersed

St. Peter's Basilica, the Vatican.

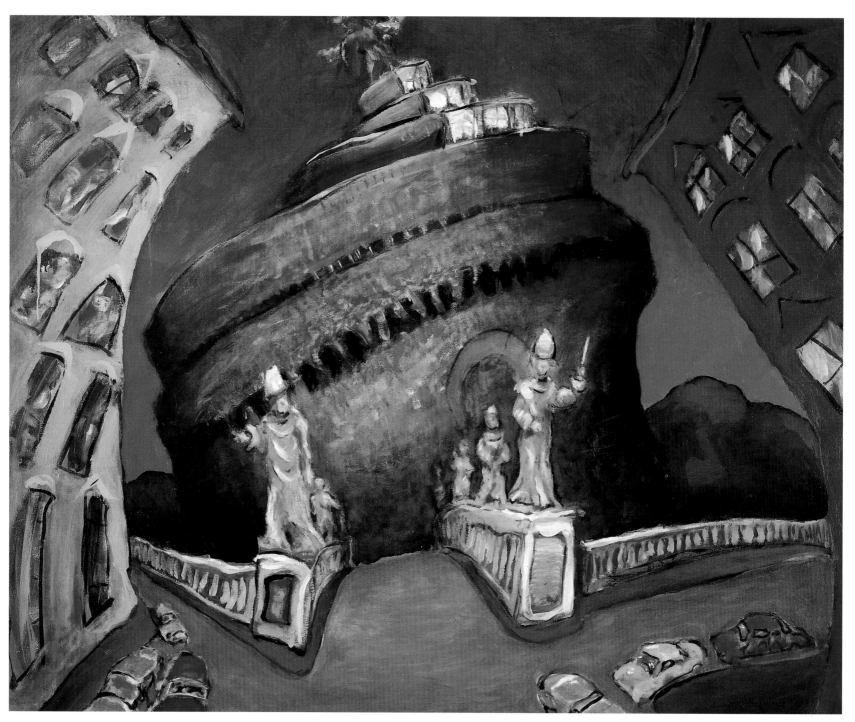

Rome: Castle Sant' Angelo, oil on canvas, 59 x 48 inches.

[LEFT] Rome's Castle Sant' Angelo.
[BELOW] *Rome: Castle Sant' Angelo*, pen and ink.

Jewish and Christian survivors like dandelion seeds scattered before a wild summer storm. Rome, that banned both faiths from the Holy City for long, painful years.

Part of the answer to the question has to do with the fact that Jerusalem and the Holy Land were virtually inaccessible to Christians for centuries. Rome became a kind of holy substitute that Christians turned to as their destination. Yet, that practical answer is only partially complete. An explanation more appreciative of spiritual reasons brings us back to the phrase: *Ad limina apostolorum!* Above all else, Rome is considered holy, and is revered and visited by faithful Christians, precisely because it is the city where the great Apostles of the faith—Peter and Paul—gave their witness to Christ. In Rome, the imperial capital itself, they boldly bore witness to their faith in Jesus, the Christ. In Rome their witness (in Greek, "martyrdom") was ultimately given by the shedding of their blood in imitation of Jesus, their Lord. In Rome the martyred Apostles lie to this day, venerated by the Christians who visit their glorious tombs, the thresholds of the Apostles. That, primarily, is why Christians still make pilgrimages to the city called Eternal.

Gloriously martyred Peter and Paul were by no means Rome's only claim to glory. Another of Rome's ancient

[ABOVE] *Vatican Piazza*, pen and ink.

[OPPOSITE] *Vatican: Scala Reggia*, oil on canvas, 48 x 59 inches.

titles is "City of Martyrs": Rome can claim hundreds of them, some honored as the greatest heroes of the Christian faith. Men, women and even children, when faced with furious persecution, chose to remain faithful to Christ. Rather than betray their Lord and his Church, they died in the flesh, trusting that their lives would continue in Christ.

Many of the early Christian martyrs went to their gruesome deaths singing hymns of praise to God for the privilege of sharing in Christ's saving death. Some died speaking words of forgiveness and pardon, reenacting Jesus' own words for his Roman executioners: "Father, forgive them. They know not what they do." And to the astonishment of many, those condemned to die due to religious intolerance and fear inspired their very persecutors' conversions to the faith. As the African churchman Tertullian astutely observed, "the blood of the martyrs is the seed of the Church." The more they were mocked, mistreated, tortured and slain, the greater the serene Christians' moral and spiritual impact on the spectators and imperial officials. Throughout the empire, Romans and non-Romans alike converted to the Christian faith in steadily growing numbers, despite the constant risk of death. Nothing like this martyr-driven conversion of the masses had ever been seen before.

To understand how central this veneration of the martyrs has been to the idea of Christian pilgrimage to Rome, one need only reflect on how many well-known sites in Rome have connections to martyrdom. Saint Peter's Basilica, for example, was not constructed by the Emperor Constantine to be a functioning church for regular worship, nor as the pope's cathedral or head of government, but as a *martyrium* (a shrine built over a martyr's grave). The basilica and the adjoining Vatican grew in liturgical and papal importance only slowly, as the papacy itself took on ever-greater significance within the Church. The same is true for the basilicas of Saint Paul,

The Piazza and Basilica of St. Peter's, Rome.

St Peter's Basilica Prayer

Awesome is this place.

Awesome is the hand of this poor fisherman

That continues to reach out with his net

For a great catch.

Great is the voice that speaks

From this tomb of your martyr Peter.

Give more hands and more voices

To serve the needy

And to shout your love.

Saint Lawrence and Saint Agnes—all subtitled "Outside the Walls," since the martyrs' graves they honored were all located outside the walls of the inhabited city, as stipulated by Roman burial law.

The Basilica of the Holy Cross in Jerusalem, built by Constantine's mother, Empress Helena, was also constructed to house a martyr's relics, in this case, the precious "trophies" of Jesus' own death and burial. Jesus, after all, was the prototype of all Christian martyrs. The Christian empress returned from her relic-seeking expedition in Jerusalem with the true cross, the crown of

Some months ago I made a request to the secretariat of the Vatican to accept us for a private mass with the pope. Having heard nothing in response, I figured the letter had been put into a convenient file and forgotten. However, much to our surprise and delight, I received a formal invitation which was delivered to our porter's office this evening. It is for tomorrow morning at the great door to the Scala Regia in St. Peter's square. How exciting!

I can barely sleep for fear that I won't hear the alarm and will miss the mass. But when 5:30 finally comes around, I stagger out of my bed and quickly ready myself to go. (There isn't too much to do when you wear a religious habit!) I run outside and am whisked by a cab to the Vatican. On the stroke of 6:45 the door opens, and each person is called from the list that a major-domo is holding. The Swiss guards are waiting in the hall as we begin our walk through the courtyard of St. Damasus and into another building. We are put into elevators that take us to the top floor of the papal palace, and are led into a rather small little chapel to have mass. Pope John-Paul II is kneeling in front of the altar where he has been praying, I am told, for about two hours.

As I pray, I think of the man in front who hears the cries of all humanity, whether it is from natural disasters or from humanity's own sinfulness. He hears the cries of the Rwandans, the Guatemalans, the Venezuelans. He knows more about the events of our earth than perhaps any other leader. I am in awe.

After the ceremony, we return to the adjacent room, which I recognize from the many television pictures I have seen. It is his working office—where he has received President Gorbachev of the former Soviet Union, and American presidents Ronald Reagan, Jimmy Carter, George Bush and Bill Clinton. He has met with heads of state from Israel, Palestine, Tibet and so many others that his days are a constant flow from one person to another. Some carry messages of peace. Others ask for help in bringing peace about. And here I am standing in a receiving line as the pope enters, welcomes us all, and then goes from one to another, asking our name and what brings us here. (Next to me is an Italian missionary who has worked for fifty years in the slums of India!)

I look at this face, which is perhaps the best known face in the world. It is kindly and peaceful, with eyes that penetrate deep into the person. This man moves very slowly and is stooped, yet has a lively intelligence and spirit. The Holy Father stops in front of me and says: "Aah, a Benedictine! Where are you from?" I say, "Collegeville," and he says, "Oh yes, wonderful liturgy!" He blesses me. I notice while he is greeting other people that the art in the room is all contemporary work done in these last few years. The paintings create a wonderful atmosphere for working or talking. Obviously someone has good taste. After moving through the whole room he asks us to remember him in our prayers, and the audience is over.

[ABOVE] *Teatro di Marcello*, watercolor, 28 x 20 inches.

[OPPOSITE] *Teatro di Marcello*, oil on canvas, 59 x 48 inches.

thorns, the nails and the title (I.N.R.I) that hung over Jesus' head. To house these priceless relics, she converted her own imperial residence into a church, filling the lowest level of the foundations with soil excavated in the holy city. To visit Helena's church was, in a sense, to visit Jerusalem itself, and for centuries the pope's solemn procession to that church during Holy Week was described simply as "to Jerusalem."

Even sites most tourists consider to be of purely archaeological or historical importance are often connected to the martyrs. The Roman Coliseum, for example, is sacred to Christians for the blood the early Christians spilled on the amphitheater's sand, as they provided entertainment for Rome's citizens. While the Circus Maximus was made familiar as the site of Charlton Heston's dramatic chariot race scene in the movie *Ben Hur*, few know that more Christians were martyred in the Circus Maximus than in the Coliseum. Piazza Navona is perhaps best known to tourists for its famous Bernini *Fountain of the Four Rivers*, its outdoor cafés, restaurants, chocolate truffle ice cream and omnipresent

[ABOVE] Rome's Piazza Navona.
[RIGHT] *Rome: Piazza Navona*,
oil on canvas, six panels, 90³/₈ x 72¹/₄ inches.

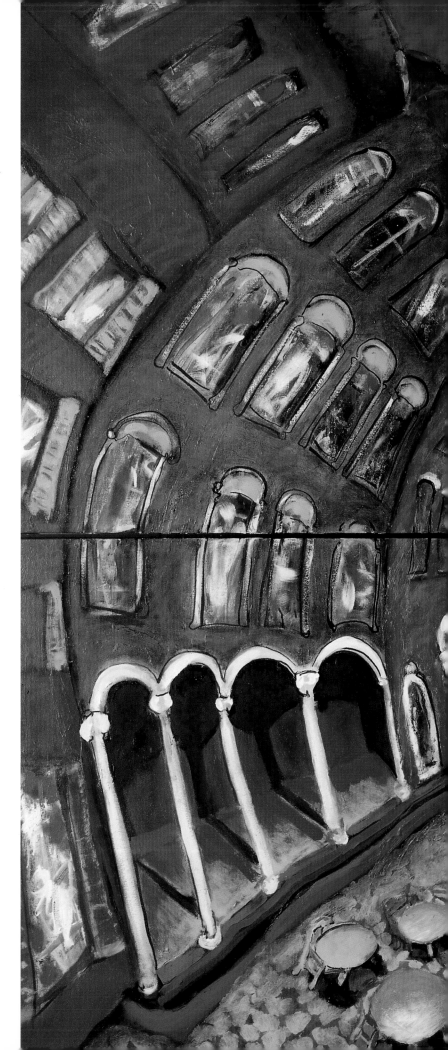

Rome: Basilica of Mary Major, oil on canvas, 76 x 63 inches.

HERE IN THIS FORUM OR MARKET PLACE OF THE IMPERIAL ROMANS I SEE THE MAGNIFICENCE OF A PAST LOVINGLY PRESERVED. LIKE MILLIONS WHO HAVE LIVED HERE AND MILLIONS WHO HAVE PASSED BY I AM AWED. HUMAN SPIRITS CREATED, BUILT AND SUSTAINED THESE PHYSICAL MARKS OF PAST GENERATIONS. PILLARS OF OUR PAST, WHERE ARE YOU? PILLARS OF OUR FAITH, PILLARS OF OUR MINDS, PILLARS OF OUR LOVE— WHERE HAVE YOU HIDDEN?

Rome: Basilica of Mary Major, watercolor, 38 x 28 inches.

ROME: 8/27/99

The eternal city, with gates so high and with so many paths that lead into and out of every portal; the via Appia, Nomentana and many others—all are busy night and day with noisy, laughing, busy Romans going about life. The great basilicas: St. Mary Major, St. John Lateran, St. Susanna, and St. Paul, all take in a stream of humanity remembering the apostles and the first martyrs. These crowds are especially large at the Flavian Arena, Colosseum and Vatican City. But they are all searching for one common thread: peace, serenity and hope for the future. Many of these generations have disappeared, yet the legacy left here is rich in architecture and art. But beyond these stones I am looking for something that goes even deeper, and that is the message of a young Jew and his friends.

I don't know how often I have drawn or painted here in the ancient Forum. Each time, I get a deeply earthy feeling as I draw the pillars, statues or ruins. It seems so elementary: the birth of this city in the eighth century B.C., its growth to become the superpower of the known world. What grandeur and power, what spectacle and baseness! Rome grew into a thriving metropolis and then sank into oblivion for hundreds of years, as its monuments and arenas deteriorated.

Then once again, because of the Roman Church and the great art of the Renaissance and counter Reformation, this city continued to grow and thrive to become one of the great cities of the world. While drawing, I sense this living pulsing city. It is alive, and has a wonderful sense of contemporary design.

Rome: Altare della Patria, pen and ink.

Rome: Our Lady of Victory Plaza, oil on canvas, 59 x 48 inches.

caricature artists. Yet it is also the site where young Agnes willingly and bravely died for Christ rather than lose her consecrated virginity. Indeed, there are few plots of ground in Rome that have not been stained crimson by the blood of the martyrs, making the city inestimably dear to the Christian pilgrim.

Over the centuries, the former capital of a pagan empire was transformed into the capital of a new Christian one. After the pagan empire's collapse in the late fifth century, the populace turned to the successor of

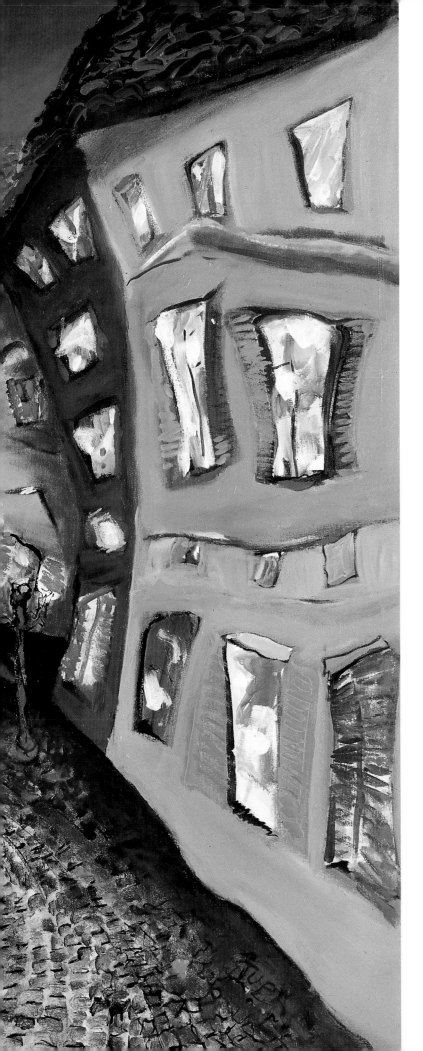

the Apostles Peter and Paul, the Bishop of Rome. With affection the Romans called him Papa, and much of the former imperial administration and leadership then came to be exercised by the people's spiritual father. Rome once again became the *caput mundi* (head of the world), but now it was the head of the Christian world. Pilgrims thronged to the thresholds of the Apostles and the martyrs, as well as a large number of sacred sites such as the catacombs, churches and shrines that honored countless newer saints. In 1887, archaeologist Mariano Armellini catalogued 959 churches in Rome, not counting the 497 known to have already disappeared by 1870, and another forty-eight shortly thereafter. In 1993, Ferruccio Lombardi cataloged 416 existing churches in Rome built between A.D. 313 and 1925; 314 of them were within the city walls, and 106 in the various regions nearby.

In addition to sacred Rome, there are vestiges of a variety of "Romes" to be found everywhere in the city's current incarnation. One can visit remains of the original settlement of Rome on the Palatine Hill, whose 753 B.C. founding is attributed to the mythic twin brothers Romulus and Remus. There are significant ruins from the fledgling city-state of Rome that was ruled by a series of kings before it experimented with the republican form of government led by "the Senate and the People." And, of course, there are the familiar monuments of Imperial Rome.

For in many ways, Rome was a city equaled by few others in the course of human history. So the awestruck visitor may perhaps take some comfort in the wisdom enshrined in the oft-repeated Italian truism, *Per Roma non basta una vita* ("A single lifetime is not sufficient to see Rome"). That in itself is a marvelous, valid reason to plan a number of visits to this city, which is unlike any other place in the world.

[LEFT] *Rome: Piazza Quirinale*, oil on canvas, 59 x 48 inches.

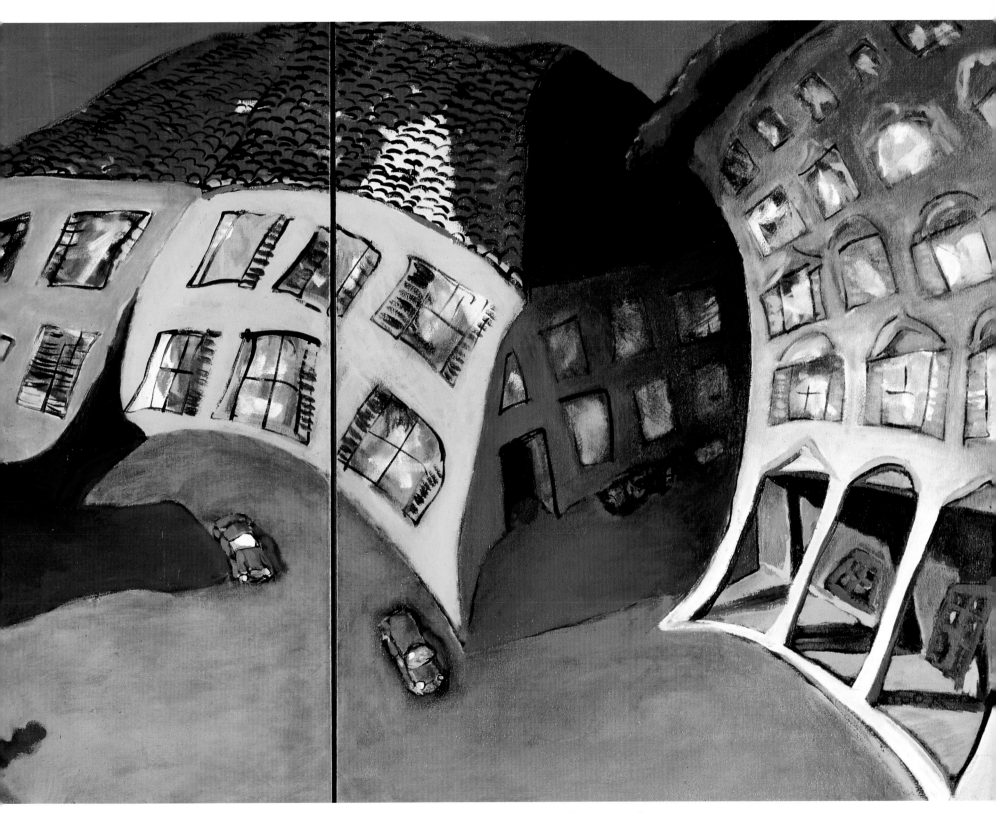

Rome: Piazza di Spagna, oil on canvas, three panels, 108 x 40 inches.

FIRST THERE WAS THE WORD, THEN THERE WAS PAINTING

FATHER JEROME TUPA CAME TO HIS VOCATION AS AN ARTIST twenty-nine years ago. His interest in what he calls "the magical world of art" was sparked by an art appreciation course at the University of North Dakota. Later, at Mayville State Teachers College in North Dakota, his passion grew under the tutelage of art professor Luella Raab Mundel.

Despite this early progress, Father Tupa remained unfulfilled. He adopted a "first-things-first" attitude, which resulted in taking his vows as a monk at St. John's Abbey in Collegeville, Minnesota. The structured life at the abbey freed his spirit and gave him a sense of purpose.

In 1968, Father Tupa graduated from St. John's with a B.A. in French and a minor in Art. In the absence of vacancies in the university's art department, the abbot steered Father Tupa toward academics, and he began his studies in French at the Sorbonne in Paris. He went on to receive three degrees: License in 1972, Maitrise in 1974, and Doctorat Troisieme Cycle (Ph.D) in 1976.

Ultimately, this intense study of the language is what led Father Tupa back to his study of painting. His understanding of art history was informed by the French, whom he described as "rich and colorful." As soon as his dissertation was completed, he began to paint in earnest, landing his first exhibition at the Librarie St. Severin in Paris.

Eventually placed in charge of the French Studies program in the university's extension in Aix-en-Provence, he spent mornings running in the hills below Mont Saint Victoire—the setting of so many of Cezanne's paintings. Thus inspired, Father Tupa began to create mountainous landscapes filled with trees and light. At the end of the year, the paintings were exhibited in Aix and created a local stir with their uncommon American perspective.

In 1982 Father Tupa returned to St. John's to be ordained in the priesthood and receive his Master of Divinity Degree from the School of Theology. During these years he painted what he calls "inner shapes and colors," exhibiting often in California, Texas, Arizona, Colorado and Minnesota.

But it was his sabbatical year in 1987 that provided " a whole new inspiration,"—the intense colors and ancient textures of Rome. This prolific period produced a series of thirty-five paintings known as the *Feu d'Artifices*. They emerged from his meditations on the image of a couple dancing, and how this connected to "the workings of the larger world." He saw the whole world as engaged in dance: "On the surface this may sound trivial, yet theologically and artistically it is vital to my understanding of how one might develop a new iconography for Christians." Then, upon his return to Saint John's University, he "hit a wall. Everything I painted turned to mud." Still he continued to paint the dance until his persistence resulted in a major breakthrough. "I just made a high circle on the canvas. With one gigantic stroke, I moved into abstract painting."

What followed was a series of thirty circle-based paintings entitled *Sentinels of Fire*. Father Tupa saw the orbs as "both soothing and healing through their intensity… where a viewer could find an overwhelming sense of peaceful calm." Not coincidentally, his first completely abstract works were initially conceived as homage to the Abstract Expressionist Mark Rothko. Containing figurative forms charged with sexuality and paradox, these works were born of Father Tupa's own physical, intellectual and emotional conflicts.

The orb series, a group of massive and predominantly "masculine" paintings, had its first major exhibition at the Minnesota Museum of Art in 1990. They were shown alongside paintings from the concurrent *Goddess* series. The *Goddesses* were, as Father Tupa noted, "Vulnerable, in need of healing power I had sought in the *Sentinels of Fire*." Inspired by Bernini's *The Ecstasy of Saint Theresa*, they depict collapsed and bleeding female figures. These paintings explore the conflicting emotions experienced by a humanity "sorely in need of the love of God."

Tired of the reds that had dominated his recent bleeding *Goddess* and *Sentinels of Fire* series, Father Tupa turned to a palette of grays for his next works, the *Inscription* series. He drew inspiration from his earlier experiences in Italy, when he spent time wandering the catacombs near Rome—underground sepulchers inscribed with elaborate graffiti. The *Inscription* series celebrates the rediscovery of the catacombs in 1578, and their reopening in the nineteenth century.

Following this period of spiritual broadening, Father Tupa's work exploded, both in form and in brushwork. While the *Sentinels of Fire* appeared primordial and molten, his new *Eye of the Needle* works had flickering surfaces.

After completing the *Eye of the Needle* series, Father Tupa immediately began another. The monumental *Eclipse* series reassembled "masculine" and "feminine" forms to suggest the attraction and balance of opposites. At the same time, he was also working on a series of sixty oil pastels, the *Memoire* series. Seeds of the *Road to Rome* series can be found here: the inscription of the first pastel, taken from words Father Tupa saw on a catacomb wall: *Petrus et Paulus Provictore* (Peter and Paul the first to overcome).

In 1991, Father Tupa began his *Pilgrimage* series. Unlike *Road to Rome*, these works were not created from a physical journey, but an emotional one that created a simple structure for the paintings: obelisks. With pointed tops and slender sides, their symbolic center represented the presence of God. The subjects included tortoise shells with the same flowing geometric pattern that Father Tupa perceived in his own style. By the time the series ended, the work had become completely abstract.

With a commission to paint all the Californian missions, Father Tupa set out in a new artistic direction. His internal quest shifted to an exploration of the very physical presence of the missions. The *Californian Mission* and the *Road to Rome* series have much in common. Both involve a physical journey to individual sites, where watercolors and drawings were made in preparation for larger studio works. Both share a bright, sunny palette and flowing, bending forms. In turn, the *Road to Rome* has now led to a new pilgrimage-based series—*Santiago de Compostela*.

Father Tupa's career as a painter reveals him to be a man who has always sought an answer to the artist's most persistent question: How do you do something new? Or rather, how can you create a fresh vision that is as spiritually inspiring as works of the past? Always one to speak to spiritual issues, Father Tupa has actively sought out a new iconography for painting.

Father Tupa's art celebrates his relationship with the world, and with God. His paintings are an invitation to partake of and share in this balanced wholeness. In this process, he fills the viewer with what he recognizes as "our deepest strivings," those of "completion, and love."

MARK KRISCO

Rome: San Gregorio, pen and ink and color crayon.

WITHOUT THE GENEROUS HELP AND FRIENDSHIP of the following people, I could not have completed this project. I am grateful to Mark Krisco for his excellent work (and words); John Pellegreene for, among many other things, his expert advice; Gail Dorn for her belief in the value of this project; Maureen Wright for all her support and input; Bart Bartholomew for his fabulous photographs; and Lena Tabori and Katrina Fried for their diligence in seeing this project to its wonderful conclusion.

Also, a special thank you to Marshall Field's and the Target Foundation for their generous support.

FATHER JEROME TUPA